Media in an Authoritarian State

A Study of Myanmar

Manish Kumar

ATLANTIC

PUBLISHERS & DISTRIBUTORS (P) LTD

Published by

ATLANTIC

PUBLISHERS & DISTRIBUTORS (P) LTD

7/22, Ansari Road, Darya Ganj, New Delhi-110002
Phones : +91-11-40775252, 23273880, 23275880, 23280451
Fax : +91-11-23285873
Web : www.atlanticbooks.com
E-mail : orders@atlanticbooks.com

Branch Office
5, Nallathambi Street, Wallajah Road, Chennai-600002
Phones : +91-44-64611085, 32413319
E-mail : chennai@atlanticbooks.com

ISBN 978-81-269-1944-4

Printed in India at Glorious Printers, A-13, D.S.I.D.C.,
Jhilmil Industrial Area, Delhi-110095

Preface

This work is a product of my half a decade's research on the society and media in Myanmar. As a student of Sociology and Mass Communication, I have been closely interested in interlinking these two disciplines; and as a result, have focused on the study of society from the lense of mass media. As a fourth pillar of democracy, media acts as a mirror of the society and it has played such a significant role in creating awareness and dissemination of information in matured democracies. But the role of mass media remains highly restricted and circumscribed in non-democratic societies. This is largely a result of the authority structure of the regime under which the media is functioning. It is this very important issue which I have sought to analyse in the present study. How does the authority structure operationalise the role of mass media in an authoritarian regime and its role in the democratization process is the research question which I have put forward. The case of Myanmar has been taken as a model to analyse the role of mass media in an authoritarian regime. Recent regime transition and political reforms being initiated in the country for establishment of a liberalized media provided me an opportunity to understand the transition which is taking place in the field of mass media as well. It should, however, be mentioned here that mass media has also played an important role as agenda setter for democratic reforms in the country. Particular mention can be made of the foreign and the exiled media in the case of Myanmar.

Myanmar had relatively sophisticated press environments in Asia before independence. The military coup of 1962 has forced the government to shut down publications and take action against journalists that were deemed a threat to national security. There are numerous accounts of journalists who have been jailed, tortured, killed or exiled using the Printers and Publishers Registration Act (1962) and Television and Video Law (1985).

In Myanmar today, the traditional media is completely controlled by the state, including three newspapers, three TV stations, two radio stations, and one news agency.

Constant threats and intimidation have circumscribed the media in Myanmar, but now under the leadership of the reform-minded President, Thein Sein, the restrictions on media are being lifted.

Myanmar, being a close neighbour to India also wants political reforms and national reconciliation. Here, only the free press can bring about social change.

Manish Kumar

Acknowledgements

A study of this magnitude and on such a restricted topic in Myanmar would not have been possible without the help of exiled media group and other people from Myanmar staying in New Delhi. In this regard, I am grateful to the members of Mizimma News, Democratic Voice of Burma and NDTV for focusing on Myanmar. The insights given by Dr. Tint Swe (NCGUB), Soe Myn, Thin Thin (Mizimma), and Nye Nye (Democratic Voice of Burma) have been really helpful. I am indebted to scholars and activists: Aung Naing Oo (Vahu Development Initiative), Myo Win (Smile Foundation, Yangon), Khin Zaw Win (Tampadipa Institute, Yangon), Salai Isaac Khen (The Gender and Development Initiative, Yangon), Shwe Shwe Sein Latt (Creative Home, Yangon), Khin Ohmar (Burma Partnership), and Aung Marm Oo (Arakan Human Rights and Development Organisation). I am also grateful to Burma Centre Delhi, Burma Centre Prague and Euro Burma Office, New Delhi for regular updates and interactions on the upcoming developments in the country. My recent interaction with the political activists Zin Mar Aung (Yangon School of Political Science), and Fergus Eckersley (British Embassy in Yangon) has been really encouraging. They have helped me in understanding the recent political developments and current period of change and transition in Myanmar. Customary interactions with Myanmar watchers in New Delhi have also helped me in deepening my understanding and knowledge about politics and society in Myanmar. Last but not least, I would like to express my deepest appreciation to all those who have directly or indirectly facilitated and helped me in completing this study entitled *Media in an Authoritarian State: A Study of Myanmar*. An honourable mention goes to my family and friends for their understanding and support in completing this study.

Although the name was changed from Burma to Myanmar in 1989, yet with all due apologies to the pro-democracy activists and all my Burmese friends, I have preferred to use the name Myanmar as it is officially called, notwithstanding the solidarity with the Burmese cause. However, I take full responsibility for all errors and omissions in this study.

Manish Kumar

List of Tables and Figures

Acronyms

ABMA	All Burma Monks Alliance
AFPFL	Anti-Fascist People's Freedom League
AMIC	Asia Media Information and Communication Centre
AMRDP	All Mon Region Democracy Party
ANFREL	Asia Network for Free and Fair Elections
ASEAN	Association of Southeast Asian Nations
BBC	British Broadcasting Corporation
BDA	Burma Defence Army
BEWG	Burma Environment Working Group
BGF	Border Guard Force
BIA	Burma Independence Army
BNA	Burma National Army
BNHR	Burma Network for Human Rights
BNI	Burma News International
BP	Burma Partnership
BSPP	Burma Socialist Programme Party
BWS	Burmese Way of Socialism
CPB	Communist Party of Burma
CRPP	Committee Representing the Peoples' Parliament
DDoS	Distributed Denial of Service
DSI	Defense Services Institute
DVB	Democratic Voice of Burma
EBO	Euro-Burma Office
EMG	Eleven Media Group
EU	European Union
FDI	Foreign Direct Investment
HRDP	Human Rights Defenders and Promoters

HURFOM	Human Rights Foundation of Monland
IMF	International Monetary Fund
KMT	Kuomintang
KNDO	Karen National Defence Organisation
MCPC	Myanmar Core Press Council
MJN	Myanmar Journalists' Network
MJU	Myanmar Journalists' Union
MPC	Myanmar Press Council
MWJA	Myanmar Writers and Journalists Association
NCCC	National Convention Convening Committee
ND-Burma	Network for Human Rights Documentation – Burma
NDF	National Democratic Force
NED	National Endowment for Democracy
NLD	National League for Democracy
NUP	National Unity Party
ODA	Official Development Assistance
PPRL	Printers and Publishers Registration Law
PRD	Press Review Department
PSB	Press Scrutiny Board
PSRD	Press Scrutiny and Registration Division
PVO	Peoples' Voluntary Organisation
RC	Revolutionary Council
RNDP	Rakhine Nationalities Development Party
SCME	System of Correlation of Man and His Environment
SECC	Socialist Economic Construction Committee
SLORC	State Law and Order Restoration Council
SNDP	Shan Nationalities Democratic Party
SPDC	State Peace and Development Council
UEC	Union Election Commission
UMEH	Union of Myanmar Economic Holdings
UN	United Nations
USDA	Union Solidarity and Development Association
USDP	Union Solidarity and Development Party
VOA	Voice of America

Burmese Terms

Amyotha Hluttaw	House of Nationalities
Bogyoke	General
Hluttaw	Assembly
Loktha Pyithu Nezin	The Working People's Daily
Myanma Alin	The New Light of Myanmar
Myanmar Naing Ngan	Union of Myanmar
Pyidaungsu Hluttaw	Union Parliament
Pyidaungsu	Union
Pyithu Hluttaw	Peoples' Assembly
Pyithu Khit	People's Era
Sitwundans	Territorial units
Tatmadaw	Military

Contents

Chapter 1

Introduction

Myanmar had one of the least restrictive and relatively sophisticated press environments in Asia before independence. But the restrictive press laws invoked since the military coup of 1962 have forced the government to shut down publications and take action against journalists deemed a threat to national security. Myanmar is ranked 169 out of 179 nations in the world for press freedom by Reporters Without Borders, marking Myanmar one of the most press-restrictive nations in the world.[1] The roots of Burmese press freedom date to the colonial era when several newspapers played a significant role in the rise of the nationalist movement in the 1920s. By the time the Union of Burma was formed in January 1948, many prominent leaders and journalists involved in the independence movement had been assassinated, jailed, or forced into exile.

When General Ne Win seized power in March 1962, one of his first steps was to establish the Soviet-style Printers and Publishers Registration Act, which required the approval by a censor of anything that is written and distributed in the country, including all books, magazines, other periodicals, song lyrics, and motion picture scripts—in most cases before the material is distributed, and sometimes before it is printed. The government also created the Press Scrutiny Board to oversee the process of censorship. In early 1963, the government arrested the editor of the *Nation*, an outspoken defender of press freedom, and closed down the newspaper, thus, setting in motion a process that would lead to a ban on all private newspapers by December 1966. In July 1963, the military launched its own daily newspaper, *Loktha Pyithu Nezin* (*The Working People's Daily*), and formally took over another newspaper, The Guardian. In 1969, two more newspapers were nationalized including *Myanma Alin* (*The New Light of Burma*), one of the oldest newspapers in the country. In the end, only six newspapers remained, all of them owned and controlled by the military government. The government also severely restricted the import of international newspapers and magazines. In order to further prevent uncensored information from leaving the country, locally-based foreign news agencies were forced to appoint local Burmese citizens as their correspondents, and those appointments had to be approved by the government. The government retained strict control over TV and radio as well. In 1985, the Ministry of Communications, Posts, and Telegraphs enacted a special Television and Video Law that required compulsory licensing of TV sets, video machines, and satellite televisions. While it was more difficult to get access to foreign TV channels, those in Myanmar still had limited access to Burmese-language broadcasts of BBC Radio and Voice of America.

The Burmese government is one of the more successful autocratic regimes to take advantage of the 'old media model,' which lends itself to relatively easy control. The government does this through strict oversight, nationalization of media outlets, and strict censorship laws. There are numerous accounts of journalists who have been jailed, tortured, killed, or exiled using the 1962 Printers and Publishers Registration Act and 1985 Television and Video Law, including the arrest of the editor of the weekly *Myanmar Nation*, in February 2008. In Myanmar today, the traditional media are completely controlled by the state, including three newspapers, three TV stations, two radio stations, and one news agency.

However, with respect to online media, the case is different. With the emergence of the Internet during the early 1990s, the military government's media policies began to evolve in reaction to the challenges posed by the online environment. For decades, this Southeast Asian nation's reporters had been regarded as among the most restricted in the world, subjected to routine state surveillance, phone taps and censorship so intense that independent papers could not publish on a daily basis. Pre-publication censorship—applied in the past to everything from newspapers to song lyrics, fiction, poems and even fairy tales—was one of the repressive methods of control used by the military junta, which handed over power to an elected Parliament in 2011. President Thein Sein's reformist government has significantly relaxed media controls over the last year, though, allowing reporters to print material that would have been unthinkable during the era of absolute military rule—like photographs of opposition leader Aung San Suu Kyi. In its recent move, the new regime has announced that the news and religious publications would no longer be required to submit stories for review to state censors before publication, ending one part of its decades-old grip on information.[2]

1.1 OBJECTIVE OF THE STUDY

This study is an attempt to study the role of mass media in an authoritarian state of Myanmar. It explores the social and political fabric of the nation and tries to study the authority structure within which mass media operates in the country. The objective of the study has been outlined below:

1. To study the character of mass media in an authoritarian state.
2. To explore various theories of media and its application in the case of Myanmar.
3. Examine the role of mass media in pressurizing and creating awareness in the international community about the authoritarian structure of the regime in Myanmar.
4. Finally, to study the responsibility of mass media in setting the agenda for reforms after transition from authoritarianism to democracy.

1.2 HYPOTHESIS/RESEARCH QUESTION

Structure of mass media in an authoritarian regime like Myanmar is the core issue which this study seeks to explore.

This has been outlined in the research questions mentioned below.

1. How far does the mass media help in understanding the social and political fabric of a nation?
2. To what extent authority structure of a regime determines the framework of mass media in a country?
3. What has been the impact of mass media in persuading the international community for reforms within Myanmar?
4. Does the mass media set the agenda of political debate and reforms after democratization?

Mass media helps in the understanding of the autocratic military framework in Myanmar (Steinberg 2009; Callahan 2003; Fink 2001). Since 1962, the country has been ruled by military. Maung Maung Gyi (1983) has studied about the Burmese political values and socio-economic roots of authoritarianism in Myanmar. According to him, the right soil for the growth of an authoritarian system reminiscent of native Burmese monarchical rule was already present in the society. Ne Win's authoritarian political style merely cashed in on this vast store of built-in attitudes and values of Burmese society that are supportive of this rule pattern. Since then, the military has dominated the political and social system of the country. It has completely controlled all domestic media and blocked independent reporting by the foreign journalists.

Authority structure of the military regime in Myanmar has determined the framework of mass media in the country. The rule pattern of the government and persistence of patrimonial nature of the state has influenced the structure of mass media in Myanmar. In order to establish and consolidate authoritarianism, the state apparatus was based on triangular axis consisting of party machinery which relied heavily on the military for support and a highly militarized bureaucracy and police organization (Than 2007). In such a rigid authoritarian framework, there was hardly any scope for mass media to operate. There was a complete monopoly over print, broadcast and electronic media. Even censorship regulation for private media has been very strict and rigid (Zaw 2008; Leehey 2005; Allot 1993; Than 2002).

Constant threats and intimidation and surveillance have circumscribed the media in Myanmar. However, with regime's paranoia having receded under the leadership of the reform minded President Thein Sein, draconian media restrictions are gradually being lifted. In June 2011, it was announced that articles concerning sports, entertainment, technology, health and children's literature could be published without the prior approval of the censors. Previously blocked websites such as YouTube, the BBC, the Bangkok Post and the Democratic Voice of Burma (DVB) have now been made accessible. Prominent comedian and film actor such as Zarganar and DVB journalists have also been released from prison and reporters are being allowed more scope to publish critical or alternate views. Nevertheless, one challenge for research on media effects in authoritarian regimes is data availability. Authoritarian regimes rarely permit independent survey research and when they themselves conduct public opinion surveys the results are often not made public. Thus, with some exceptions reliable micro-level data on public opinion in authoritarian regimes are not readily available.

Mass media, particularly, the exiled media, foreign portals and blogs have played a significant role in persuading for reforms in Myanmar. Foreign media such as British Broadcasting Corporation (BBC)—Burma Service, Voice of America (VOA), Democratic Voice of Burma (DVB) and other exiled media houses have kept the issue of democracy in Myanmar alive in the international politics. International community has stressed the need for political reforms and national reconciliation in the new regime. Recently, the issue of Rohingya community in Myanmar has also attracted international interest and has widely been covered by the foreign media, blogs and social networking sites. International community is stressing the need to end the violence, to grant full humanitarian assistance to the areas affected, to allow the displaced communities to safely return to their homes and to rehabilitate them.

Mass media often serves as the agenda setters for political debate and reforms after democratization (Norris 2009; Du 2008). Journalists and reporters can play a multiple role in raising issues about urgent humanitarian crisis and developmental challenges facing the country. In this regard, particular mention may be made of the 2007 Saffron revolution (Ng 2008; Romano 2009; Kingston 2008; McCarthy 2008), the Constitutional Referendum held in 2008 (HRW 2008; Seekins 2009) and the elections held in 2010 (Turnell 2011; NDI 2010; ICG 2010). Media has played an important role in bringing out these issues in the public sphere and creating a wide range of political perspective for democratic deliberation. According to Habermas (1989), media—old and new—is the core institution facilitating mass communication in the public sphere in contemporary societies.

1.3 SIGNIFICANCE OF THE STUDY

It is not easy to carry out independent field survey in Myanmar's closed society. The state maintains strict surveillance over electronic communications, including e-mail, and blocks certain websites. The primary targets for blocking are political opposition or pro-democracy movements, e-mail service providers and free web space sites. Myanmar is way down the list in press freedom rankings. Although military government has relaxed visa controls and now permits foreigners to live in Myanmar for extended period, nevertheless, freedom of speech and association are still severely curtailed. Access to modern means of communication including Internet is restricted. Even possession of fax machines or satellite phones may result in lengthy imprisonment.

In the past two years, alongside other reforms, the government had begun visibly to relax its iron grip on the media, allowing coverage of previously taboo topics such as Ms. Suu Kyi and her National League for Democracy. With the abolition of pre-publication censorship, as recently announced, editors are exempt from submitting material to the Press

Scrutiny and Registrations Department for approval before printing. But this does not mean that the Myanmar media is now free to report on the remaining 13 directives and six instructions mentioned in the 1962 Printers and Publishers Registration Act, imposed soon after the Ne Win coup. Among the subjects that remain on the sensitive list are corruption in the Army, and foreign policy. The government recently warned against reportage of the communal clashes in bordering areas.[3]

There is a serious shortage of empirical data and verifiable documentary evidence about current developments. Some foreign journalists and academics have sneaked in crossing the border illegally to observe the conditions first hand.[4] The number of students engaged in the research has grown substantially, but field surveys are still constrained and reliable sources are hard to find. For over more than thirty years, Myanmar has had no census. The last official census took place in 1983. Before that, the last credible election was held in 1931 during British rule. As a result, for years, economists, academics and researchers have relied on unreliable data.

Keeping all these limitations in view, the study has attempted to outline the structure of authoritarian regime in Myanmar and role of mass media in it. It has studied various phases of military rule and restrictions imposed upon freedom of press by the military regime. It also looks into the reform agenda of the new regime and a beginning made towards relaxations of press restrictions and censorship. This work would be useful for those who are interested in studying the role of mass media in an authoritarian system. This study sheds light on the fact the framework of mass media depends upon the social and political structure within which it operates. In the present case of Myanmar, the socio-political roots of authoritarian have played a significant role in the imposition of media restrictions and censorship. The patrimonial nature of Myanmar's society and the existence of client-patron relationship have guided the way politics has operated in Myanmar since historical periods. Thus, the political culture of authoritarianism has played a significant role in defining the structure and operation of mass media in Myanmar.

1.4 METHODOLOGY

Although much has been written about Media in Asia, yet this study would be an important contribution to the analysis of the media in an authoritarian regime such as Myanmar. The study is based on the field-work undertaken in Myanmar in 2010 to examine the role of media and the progress made towards democratization and national reconciliation. Even though at the time of my visit all the foreign media and local blogs were either banned or strictly monitored, I was able to gather some information in the course of general discussions with the local people. Mostly, people in Myanmar carry out their business on an informal discussion with a cup of tea in the evening when it is the time for the marketplaces to shut down. Most of the business dealings were based on hard cash since the lack of banking facility was a major hurdle for legitimate transfer of funds and business dealings. Up until the new reformist government took office in March last year, Myanmar's reporters had been regarded as among the most restricted in the world. Routine state surveillance which included phone taps, Internet access restrictions and other forms of censorship—including restrictions on publication of photographs of Aung San Suu Kyi—were sufficiently intense to render it impossible for independent newspapers to publish on a daily basis.

For studying the media reforms under the new regime, the study has made use of the newspapers reports, interviews and opinion surveys conducted on the refugees from Myanmar (such as pro-democracy leaders, trade union activists and journalists) staying in India.[5] The study is also based on opinion surveys and analyses of the experts on Myanmar during the course of various workshops, lectures and conferences.[6]

The study has also made use of the primary documents such as Constitutional Principles approved by the National Convention; National Convention Procedural Code; SLORC Declarations; Constitution of 'The Socialist Republic of the Union of Burma,' 1974; Constitution of the 'Union of Burma', 1947; System of Correlation of Man and Environment;

Burmese Way to Socialism; and Panglong Agreement, 1947. The report of the World Bank, UNCTAD, IMF, International Crisis Group, Human Rights Watch and Freedom House has also been used in the study. A wide range of secondary literatures on regime transition and democratisation, and on military and politics in Myanmar in the form of books, research papers, working papers, monographs and special commentaries have also been referred.

1.5 REVIEW OF THE LITERATURE

Literatures referred for the present study here fall under three thematic categories. First, covers the general review of literature on authoritarianism in general and the key elements of institutional manipulation by an authoritarian regime. Second, relates to the case study of Myanmar, particularly its hard authoritarian structure and the current phase of transition. And finally, the last theme deals with the media restrictions and reforms in Myanmar.

1.5.1 Literature on Authoritarianism

Amos Perlmutter (1981) regards authoritarianism is a system of relationships between state and society and between political and societal sources of power. It is based on a type of domination which is dependent on centralized executive control and coercion (Perlmutter 1981: 24). Andrew Heywood (2002) considers it as a belief and practice of government from above. Authoritarian regime emphasizes the claims of authority over those of individual liberty. It is also a system that is designed to infiltrate the society and isolate it from the state, so that the latter has control over the former (Heywood 2002: 38).

Greame Gill (2000) considers authoritarian regimes, by definition, not accountable or responsible in any direct, institutional fashion to the populace over whom they rule. But this does not mean that they exist in a vacuum, isolated from the population and not linked with it in any way. Every regime seeks to consolidate its position by embedding itself within the society (Gill 2000: 35). Larry Diamond (2008) argues that there is probably no country of any significant size where every single citizen regards the system of government as legitimate. Similarly, no regime, no matter how brutal and totalitarian, relies on force to survive (Diamond 2008: 89). Someone has to apply force; others have to believe in the regime. According to Diamond, even if the majority detest the political system, as in Myanmar, there are always some regime loyalists who regard the regime as legitimate and who are devoted to its defence and maintenance.

Authoritarian is distinguished from totalitarian both in degree and scope (Heywood 2002: 38). Authoritarian administration is less intrusive and not necessarily backed by the use of force. Typically, the government in an authoritarian regime is run by an elite group that uses repressive means to stay in power such as monarchical absolutism, traditional dictatorships and military rule. However, unlike totalitarian regimes, there is no desire or ideological justification for the state to control all aspects of a person's life. They tolerate a significant range of economic, religious and other freedoms. Totalitarian governments tend to be revolutionary and intend to change the basic structure of society, authoritarian ones tend to be conservative. Juan Linz's (2000) version of totalitarianism is distinguished from authoritarian systems by the use of ideology as an instrument of legitimation. Totalitarian systems possess an exclusive ideology while authoritarian systems lack an "elaborate and guiding ideology, with distinctive mentalities" (Linz 2000: 264). In its transition from authoritarianism to totalitarianism, Linz identifies a 'grey zone' between both under different nomenclatures—quasi-totalitarianism, post-totalitarianism, rationalized totalitarianism, totalitarianism without terror (Linz 2000: 240-52).

In discussing modern authoritarianism, Linz (2000: 165) and Perlmutter (1981: 2) note that one of the things upon which such regimes rest is popular mobilization. A range of bodies may be generated to organize and structure public activity including youth groups, trade unions, women groups, sporting associations, etc. The aim of such organization is to keep the people busy and to involve them in an activity which is essentially regime supporting (Gill 2000: 13). The industrial, business and the technocratic elites that emerge out of the corporatist model acts as a social support base for many conservative authoritarianism. These groups often see the 'state' as a source of substantial material support for their economic activities (*ibid.*: 15). If 'rupture' arises in this ruling class elite base, then the likely chances of transformation and transition become stronger (Diamond 2008: 90). In many cases, according to Wood (2004: 107), authoritarian regimes actually laid the institutional foundations for the subsequent rise of democracy.

According to Donald J. Porter (2002), an authoritarian regime may be a collective dictatorship, an oligarchy, or a military government. Although there has been a wide variety of authoritarian regimes historically (including one party systems, military regimes, and personal dictatorships), they all tended to be deficient in key institutional features present in liberal democracies (Porter 2002: 8). Historically, non-authoritarian regimes may take a variety of sub-forms: absolute monarchies, feudal aristocracies, fascist states, personalistic or autocratic military regimes. But according to Huntington (1991: 110), the regimes that moved towards democracy in the third wave generally fall into three groups—one party system, military regimes and personal dictatorships. Others like Pinkney (2004; 159-160), O'Niel (2006), Mc Cormick (1995: 335-336) have also adhered to this typology of authoritarian regimes. Perlmutter (1981: 130) adds one more category to it, viz. corporatist.

Andreas Schedler discusses the concept of electoral authoritarianism and how political regimes couple formal democratic institutions such as multiparty elections with authoritarian practices (*Logic of Authoritarianism*, 2006). Schedler (2010) in delineates a broad range of "menus of manipulation" in diverse institutional arenas. The new electoral authoritarian regimes of the post-Cold War have set up the full panoply of liberal-democratic institutions—from constitutions to constitutional courts, from legislatures to agencies of accountability, from judicial systems to federal arrangements, from independent media to civic associations. Most important of all, they hold regular multiparty elections at all levels of state power. In their institutional forms, these regimes are virtually indistinguishable from liberal democracies. Yet authoritarian rulers invariably compensate for these formal concessions with substantive controls. While renouncing the suppression of representative institutions, electoral authoritarian regimes specialize in their manipulation.

Authoritarianism is not peculiar to only Indonesia or Myanmar, nor solely confined to Southeast Asian region. It is prevalent throughout the world—in Africa, Latin America, East Asia, Middle East and in communist countries. But, in Southeast Asia, including Indonesia and Myanmar, authoritarianism was the way of life best known to the people of the region (Gyi 1983: v). Benedict Anderson (1983: 487) argues that the rise of New Order authoritarianism in Indonesia marks the resurrection of the state and its triumph vis-à-vis society and nation. It has been embedded in the Javanese concept of power and patrimonial authority in Indonesia (Anderson 1972) whereas in Myanmar it is a result of deep-seated belief in the Burmese political values with roots in Buddhist political and economic ideals (Steinberg 1982: 44). At the time of the withdrawal of the colonial rule, they established liberal parliamentary democracy in their respective countries. But they could not utilize the opportunities given by the liberal democratic framework and consequently within a few years of their gaining independence they reverted to authoritarianism either under civilian or military leadership (Sundhaussen 1995: 771).

1.5.2 Myanmar: Past, Present and Prospects

Andrew Sleth, in *Modern Burma Studies*, asserts that Myanmar has never been a popular subject for academic research but, since a massive pro-democracy uprising drew worldwide attention to the country in 1988, the number of scholars and students engaged in the field has grown considerably. However, they still face a number of major challenges. Along with other kinds of area studies, Burma studies have been accused by academics from the more 'scientific' disciplines of being too narrowly focused and lacking theoretical rigour. Also, it has been difficult to conduct research in Myanmar's closed society. While the latest military government has relaxed some controls, field work is still constrained and reliable sources are hard to find. Often, the knowledge gap has been filled by myths and misconceptions. Adding to these problems, since 1988 the Myanmar studies community has become highly polarised, with political and moral factors often featuring more prominently in the public debate than considered arguments based on objective analysis. According to Sleth (2010) all these factors have adversely affected modern Myanmar studies and restricted understanding of this deeply troubled country by both scholars and the wider community.

Despite the difficulty of obtaining reliable data, there has been a number of publication that examine Myanmar's economic policy during the military rule. There have been numerous works that are sociological and anthropological in nature. Numerous publications have also documented the plight of the ethnic nationalities in Myanmar. There are number of books covering the military rule and politics in Myanmar. Few of them have also looked into the socio-political roots of authoritarianism in Myanmar and have justified the continuation of the military's intervention in politics. Maung Maung Gyi in *Burmese Political Values* (1983) attempts to look at the fundamentals in the political culture of Myanmar and the trends of the authoritarian rule pattern. According to him, authoritarian attitude was found to be prevalent in the Burmese society and still exists in the society. Josef Silverstein in his book *Burma: Military Rule and the Politics of Stagnation* (1977) looks into the roots of contemporary politics and attempts to focus on institutions and processes that represent continuity and change. David Steinberg in *Burma: The State of Myanmar* (2001) deals with the crisis of 1988 and the social and political backdrop to the crisis. He focuses on this volatile state by exploring issues of authority and legitimacy in its politics, economics, social structure, and culture, since the popular uprising and military coup of 1988. Martin Smith in *Burma: Insurgency and the Politics of Ethnicity* (1999) has looked into the ethnic politics in Myanmar. He concludes that ethnic peace and political inclusiveness in Myanmar are integral pre-conditions for sustainable development and economic progress in the new century. Cristina Fink in *Living Silence* (2001) provides a wide range of survey of Burmese society. She presents the political history of the country since independence in 1948, including the 1988 nationwide pro-democracy demonstrations, the 1990 elections and more recent political developments. She also explores the remarkable range strategies and techniques which the military regime has used to maintain itself in power in defiance of the popular will. The edited volume by Ganesan, N. Kyaw Yin Hlaing (2007), *Myanmar: State, Society and Ethnicity* focuses on some of the most important and topical questions about Myanmar pertaining to issues of historical influence and political considerations that have shaped the dominant thinking within the state and the military. There are equally important studies of sensitive topics like the political economy of the state and the level of human security in the country. The three major ethnic groups in the country Karen, Kachin, and Shan are also studied in detail. Some of the negotiations between the Karen and Kachin ethnic insurgent group representatives on the one hand, and the military junta on the other, are spelled out. An important corollary finding is the importance of religion and religious personalities in brokering peace between the ethnic groups and the military government. Finally, the book deals with how the various ethnic groups are trying to cope with decades of conflict and reconstruct their communities.

The study also reviews the current situation in Myanmar and key elements of democratic transition and consolidation. In this regard, Morten B. Pedersen's chapter in *The Challenges of Transition in Myanmar* and *Southeast Asian Affairs* titled "Myanmar: Future Takes Form: But Little Changes in Sight" looks into the trends for democratisation in Myanmar. These, according to him, pose unique challenge. He also looks into the role of the international community in helping the country and its people to overcome the cultural constraints to political and economic progress. Robert Taylor in his chapter "Pathways to the Present" analyses the interconnectedness of various strands of history that have come together to shape the present. According to him, the issues which today concern the citizens of Myanmar are rooted in the country's complex and often contested institution and history. In *Southeast Asian Affairs* "Myanmar: Roadmap to Where" broad political developments and issues thrown up by the recent political changes and the current thinking of the military leadership. Mary Callahan in her chapter "Burma: Soldiers as State Builders" reviews critical points of institutional reforms and explains how these transformations have institutionalised the most durable military regime in the post-World War era. Levenstein's 2010 edited volume on Myanmar seeks to address the emerging political order and finding a way out of Myanmar's stasis. It fosters an informed discussion on how Myanmar may improve and eventually resolve its economic and political dilemmas. In an overview of Myanmar's economy, Sean Turnell asserts that prospects for the remainder of 2010 are grim. If the junta is serious about redressing the country's economic ills, Turnell proposes it implement more transparency in the privatization of industries, unify the divergent exchange rates, liberalize rice trade and agriculture, and recapitalize rural finance to restore the rural credit system. Ken MacLean writes about Myanmar's informal economy in the border regions. He finds that the various armed insurgencies, not the SPDC, are in control of these discontinuous border areas where the informal economy has thrived. Therefore, the SPDC is obliged to "co-opt" these armed insurgents in order to indirectly "govern" these areas and undercut hostilities along the border. In assessing the volatile nature of Burmese politics, Mary Callahan explains how and why military rule has endured in Myanmar. Min Zin focuses on the shortcomings of the NLD as an opposition movement. Facing perpetual coercion and repression from the regime, any opposition must resort to "alternative courses of action like public mobilization and international advocacy" to remain active. He believes that the 2010 election will introduce changes in governance that should offer some breathing room to the opposition. Since the new government will operate from the two centers of power, namely the military and the civilian government, this arrangement can produce an internal split that will offer an opportunity for "political realignment," empowering the opposition groups. Jürgen Haacke shifts the focus to Myanmar's foreign affairs and delves into the complexities of Myanmar's varied interactions with the ASEAN. Washington's new diplomatic approach toward Myanmar, Haacke judges, is one of the main reasons why ASEAN has softened its position. In contemplating international strategies applied to Myanmar, Morten B. Pedersen looks for solutions to improve its human rights situation. He recommends principled engagement, the "middle way" between ostracism and economic cooperation, as the best approach. His "middle way" involves direct engagement with "human rights practitioners and broader groups in society" and uses non-confrontational means to redress social grievances. David I. Steinberg examines the political circumstances that have influenced the United States' policy-making process toward Myanmar. The Obama administration's diplomatic strategy combines economic sanctions and practical engagement—opening a channel of dialogue with the Burmese junta.

Steinberg in *What Everybody Needs to Know About Myanmar* (2010) tries to educate the external world to the complexities that Myanmar faces and some possible avenues for alleviating its problems. He covers the recent political developments and sheds light on the complex issue that plagues the country. *Myanmar/Burma: Inside Challenges, Outside Interest* (2010) is an edited volume by Alex Rieffel. The book provides an overview of the historical and policy context and explains why positive change seemed to be possible after two decades of lost opportunities. It provides an insight into the overarching problem of national reconciliation, economic backwardness, strategic competition between India and China, nuclear question and the North Korea connection and the role of ASEAN.

A large number of research papers have also appeared in many journals. Peter Carey in his paper "From Burma to Myanmar: Military Rule and the Struggle for Democracy" studies the domestic political developments in Myanmar and the systematic destruction of nearly all the independent institutions of the state. According to him, Myanmar became the classic case of a 'weak state and strong society' and there is clearly a need for political reforms to take place in Myanmar before major economic restructuring is embarked upon. Thawnghmung in the paper "Preconditions and Prospects for Democratic Transition in Myanmar" highlights a number of changing political and economic circumstances, and examines their impact on Myanmar's 'transition to democracy'. Given the expected continuing role of the military in politics, and the pervasiveness of authoritarian practices in Burmese society, a certain level of political repression, manipulation, and restriction will likely continue for a long time. However, the empowerment and greater recognition of pro-democratic forces and civil society will at least provide more room for political manouvre and multiple checks on rampant abuses of government power. These may be able to gradually steer Myanmar toward the path of democracy. Ashley South in his paper "Political Tradition in Myanmar: A New Model for Democratisation", examines social and political transition in Myanmar and argues that re-emergence of civil society networks within and between ethnic nationality over the past decade is one of the most significant aspects of the social and political situation in the country. The author argues that while change at the national level, whether revolutionary or gradual, is urgently required, sustained democratic transition can only be achieved if accompanied by local participation. The promotion of civil society, therefore, acts as a pre-condition for democratisation in Myanmar. Herein, the author also addresses the role that foreign aid can play in supporting the re-emergence of civil society in Myanmar. Local NGOs can implement community development and humanitarian projects in border areas, in ways which build local capacities and human capital. Kyaw Yin Hlaing in his paper "Power and Factional Struggles in Post-Independence Burmese

Government" explains the ways in which power and factional struggles broke out and ended in post-independence Myanmar. Based on his study, he concludes that existence of a hegemon yields a good possibility of a stable government. Conversely, absence of such a hegemony results in an unstable government. Ruukun Katanyuu in "ASEAN's Role in Myanmar's National Reconciliation and Democratisation" analyses the factors compelling ASEAN to relax its non-interference policy regarding members and intervene in Myanmar's internal affairs. According to him, the situation in Myanmar has led ASEAN to review its policy.

The Saffron Revolution and its aftermath has been extensively covered by various research papers. Jeff Kingston in "Burma's Despair" studies the Saffron Revolution of 2007. According to him, the government's seven-step roadmap to democracy appears to have lost all credibility, and no one believes that the military or its proxies will implement the proposed constitution in good faith. Kingston views that transforming unprecedented international attention to Myanmar's plight into sustained support for alleviating severe humanitarian conditions, promoting nation building, and nurturing a time-bound dialogue for national reconciliation and democratization remains a key challenge. Andrew Sleth in "Burma's 'Saffron Revolution' and the Limits of International Influence" looks into the military government's brutal response to the latest unrest prompted an unprecedented level of diplomatic activity and a rare consensus on the need for political change. Stephan Mc Carthy in his paper "Overturning the Alms Bowl: The Price of Survival and the Consequences for Political Legitimacy in Burma" also studies the Saffron Revolution and traces the importance of Buddhism to the political legitimacy of rulers in Myanmar and examines how the authorities' relationship with the Sangha has undergone significant changes under military rule. He compares the 2007 demonstrations with earlier protests and examines how the regime's legitimacy has suffered as a result of yet another crackdown, significantly this time against demonstrations led by the largest institution outside of the *tatmadaw*.

Seekins (2009) covers the cyclone Nargis and SPDC 2008 Constitutional Referendum. Furthermore, in his 2010 article, he covers the incidence of an unwelcome visitor who visited Aung San Suu Kyi's lakeside compound in Yangon and the military regime's pretext to extend her house arrest. The article also covers the preparation for the 2010 elections and the ethnic conflict in the border areas. Turnell (2011) focuses on the dominant issue of election prevailing in the country and the release of Aung San Suu Kyi. Adoption of country's new name and flag has also been described in this paper. In his 2012 paper tiled "Myanmar in 2011: Confounding Expectations" studies the trends and transformations happening in the country after the election and the reform process being initiated.

Bissinger (2012) explores the major trends in FDI in Myanmar, focusing on changes over time in the source and sector of investment. The paper argues that over the last decade Myanmar's inward FDI has become heavily concentrated in the extractive and power sectors, while investment in manufacturing, services and other secondary and tertiary sectors has been almost non-existent. This is mostly the result of a poor investment climate, including import and export regulations, a weak judicial system, currency controls and weak property rights. The paper shows that China, Hong Kong, South Korea and Thailand have been the main investors in Myanmar, while Singapore, India and Western countries invested little in the 2000s. This divergence is driven partly by the differing investment patterns of the source countries, yet also reflects commercial and geopolitical realities, sanctions and concerns over energy security. The paper then examines whether and how FDI can lead to economic development in Myanmar, and closes by discussing the importance of recent political and economic reforms for rebalancing Myanmar's FDI. Davies (2012) explores the reasons for the ineffectiveness of ASEAN in influencing Myanmar. These are found in the normative and institutional architecture of ASEAN, specifically its lack of punitive sanction-based compliance mechanisms. According to the author, ASEAN has been engaged in a strategy of rhetorical action to promote compliance with regional standards which lacks a coherent political strategy. This article suggests that correcting this shortcoming through the development of greater coherence is achievable within the existing ASEAN approach to managing regional affairs.

The book has also covered the report of ICG titled "Myanmar: How Strong is the Military Regime". The report studies the strengths and vulnerabilities of the SPDC regime and addresses the prospects for non-violent democratic transition in the country and ways to achieve that transition. ICG in another report titled "Myanmar: After the Crackdown" studies the violent crushing of protests led by Buddhist monks in Burma/Myanmar in late 2007. According to the report, the immediate challenges are to create a more durable negotiating process between government, opposition and ethnic groups and help alleviate the economic and humanitarian crisis that hampers reconciliation at all levels of society. The massive devastation caused by cyclone Nargis has been covered by ICG Report of 2008. According to the report, while 'humanitarian' aid is a reasonable response to a temporary emergency, the deepening structural crisis in Myanmar demands a response of a different type and magnitude. The international community should commit unequivocally not only to helping Myanmar recover from the destruction of Nargis, but also to making up for years of neglect and helping move the country forward. This means much more aid. Equally importantly, it means different aid, aimed at raising income and education as well as health levels, fostering civil society, improving economic policy and governance, promoting the equality of ethnic minorities and improving disaster prevention and preparedness.

The ICG Briefing on Myanmar Elections (May 2010) updates recent developments, including an analysis of the electoral legislation issued in March. The National Democratic Institute (NDI) report of August 2010 regards the Electoral framework as fundamentally undemocratic. ICG in its March 2011 Briefing covers the 2010 elections and the post-election landscape. It reflects the continued dominance of the old order with the president and one of the two vice presidents drawn from its ranks and a number of cabinet ministers recycled. Nevertheless, it would be a mistake to conclude that nothing has changed. The top two leaders of the former military regime have stepped aside, and a new generation has taken over. A new constitution has come into force, which fundamentally reshapes the political landscape, albeit in a way that ensures the continued influence of the military. A number of technocrats have been brought into the cabinet, and at the local level ethnic groups now have at least some say in the governance of their affairs. In 2012 Briefing, ICG has covered the one year of reforms in Myanmar. One year into the new semi-civilian government, Myanmar has implemented a wide-ranging set of reforms as it embarks on a remarkable top-down transition from five decades of authoritarian rule. Although after the bye-elections of April 2012, NLD emerged as the largest opposition party, yet this does not alter the balance of power, given that only a small percentage of seats were contested, but it is of major symbolic importance, as it has the potential to inject greater dynamism into political life.

According to ICG Report 2012 on economic reforms, along with sweeping political reforms, Myanmar has embarked on an ambitious program of economic changes, aimed at rebuilding its moribund economy and integrating it with the global system. It has begun a managed float of the currency, and is dismantling the old system of monopolies and privileged access to licenses, permits and contracts. These changes will have a big impact on the entrenched economic elite—crony businessmen, the military and former political heavyweights linked to the government party. Unanticipated economic shocks, social unrest or political uncertainty in the lead-up to the next elections in 2015 all represent potential risks to that stability. But if it is able to manage this complex process, Myanmar has the possibility to finally realise its enormous economic potential, catching up with its neighbours while avoiding some of their mistakes.

1.5.3 Media in Myanmar

Four Theories of Press (1963) seek to explore, why is the press as it is? Why does it apparently serve different purposes and appears in widely different forms in different countries? Why, for example, is the press of the Soviet Union so different from United States and so on. According to this book, one of the most primary reasons for these differences is the coloration of the social and political structure within which it operates. It reflects the system of social control whereby the relations of individuals and institutions are adjusted. Thus, in order to see the differences between press systems in full perspective, one must look at the social systems in which the press functions. Corresponding to the origin of mass communication, in the Renaissance, authors in this book have identified four basic theories of press, viz. the authoritarian and its modification—the Soviet Communist theory; the Libertarian theory and its medication—the Social Responsibility theory. Working within the notion of the democratic public sphere, Norris and Odugbemi (2009) emphasize the institutional or collective roles of the news media as watchdogs over the powerful, as agenda-setters calling attention to social needs in natural and man-made disasters and humanitarian crisis, and as gatekeepers incorporating a diverse and balanced range of political perspectives and social actors. Each, the authors argue, is vital for making democratic governance work in an effective, transparent, inclusive, and accountable manner. Romano (2009) in *Asian Journalism* describes some of the over-arching issues that affect the journalists' contributions to governance and democracy in the world's most populous continent, while also recognizing the diversity of cultural, religious, economic, political and media systems between and within Asian nations.

Allott (1993) covers the era of complete censorship in Myanmar. She begins with a brief historical and political background and the role of media before the imposition of military rule in 1962. System of control over publishing after passing of the Printers' and Publishers' Registration Act in 1962 has also been elaborated by the author. Burmese writers work in an atmosphere of uncertainty and apprehension. The only way for a writer to address one or more of the many taboo subjects is through the construction of metaphors, and, in resorting to these, she or he can only hope that the veiled meaning will be discerned by the reader, but not by the censor. In *Writing in a Crazy Way*, Leehey (2005) discusses the difficulties of self-expression and a sense of personal identity within the framework of a militarized public domain. The author describes the refusal of a particular school of writers to publish work that conforms to the regimes' ideological dictates. Leehey studies the changing value of intellectuals under the BSPP and subsequent regimes. Than (2002) in "Meeting Market Challenges in the Shadow of the State" illustrates how market dynamics have brought changes to the form and substance of the media. He focuses on how editors and journalists have harnessed the state's market reform agenda to bring significant changes to a rigidly controlled media. The author has covered the evolution of the media in Myanmar in a historical perspective and the current challenges faced by it. According to him, the extent to which the media acts as a communication medium is largely determined by the groups that have control over them. In case of Myanmar, this control has been state's prerogative for nearly four decades, since the military coup in 1962. Nancy Hudson Rodd in her book chapter titled "Not a Rice Eating Robot", *Freedom to Speak in Burma* (2008) covers the brief political history of Myanmar before beginning a detailed discussion on the censorship rules and restrictions on freedom of expression. According to the author, although the military regime "restricts the citizen's access to independent information but imposes and reproduces their version of Myanmar on billboards, newspapers, radio and television broadcasts and publications" (p. 91). The author further explains the plight of the international media covering Myanmar such as BBC, VOA, RFA, DVB and the great odds suffered by the authors, film-makers, poets, cartoonists and journalists "who are continually trying to write between the lines of prohibition and inquire into open spaces for the truth to be expressed in Burma" (p. 101).

Martin Smith in Country Report of Article 19 titled *State of Fear: Censorship in Burma*, examines the historical development of the country's media and draconian press restrictions (1991). In his 1995 report, he reviews recent developments in Myanmar and their impact on the right to freedom of expression at a time of economic transition. The report presents, the quickening pace of economic development in 1990s however, these have been little more than cosmetic. According to the report, far-reaching reform is still urgently needed if the current political impasse is really to be ended and the country's burgeoning social and humanitarian problems are to be addressed. The international community too, including Asian and Western governments alike, has a key responsibility to ensure that such reform does occur before Myanmar is permitted to take its rightful place as a respected member of that community.

Brooten (2006) studies the situation facing journalists from Burma (Myanmar) living in exile in Thailand. This article explores the consequences of political violence on the development of indigenous journalism in a multiethnic state. Although influenced by the recent surge in foreign funding, these journalists struggle to develop a context-specific model for their work, calling into question the relevance of the dominant U.S. approach to 'objectivity'. The contested nature of concepts such as unity, independence, and censorship in these often high-risk areas suggests the need for a more complex model of media development in contexts of political violence. Myay (2011) discusses the absence of media freedom which is one of the major challenges for democratization process in Myanmar. She highlights the need for emergence of new media to pave the way for propaganda with messages and information related to democracy and for the public good. The paper covers the background history and media control by military government in Myanmar. Military junta has been keen on carrying out its propaganda to persuade poorly educated and vulnerable people mostly from rural areas. The information provides to the public by country's mass media including newspapers, TV, journals and magazines are intended for propaganda only. She argues that the countervailing forces by citizens and pro-democracy groups can utilize new media for anti-propaganda of military government. Chowdhary (2008) examines the root causes, progress, and outcomes of the Saffron Revolution and attempts to parse out the extent to which technology may have played a useful or detrimental role in the unfolding of events. The uprising in Myanmar is ultimately an example of a protest where digitally network technologies played a critical role, but where the protests failed to lead to major political change. As discussed at the end of this paper, the lasting impact of the protests is debatable, and potentially both positive and negative. However, a unique aspect of Burmese transnational mobilization is that individual bloggers and digital activists worked together with permanent advocacy organizations with full-time staff such as the Myanmar Campaign UK or US Campaign for Burma. This combination of online and offline groups acting together is likely to have a more significant and sustained impact than purely online movements, which may have a more limited attention span.

1.6 STRUCTURE OF THE BOOK

This book looks into the regime structure of an authoritarian state and examines the role of mass media in it. The case study of Myanmar has been chosen here, simply because of the transition taking place in the country and the numerous challenges faced by the current regime in coping up with the internal as well as external pressures. The role of mass media was highly circumscribed during the military rule for over more than six decades. But in the wake of the recent process of reforms and changes taking place in Myanmar, some of those restrictions have given way to a more open and free mass-media regime. Nevertheless, the prevailing autocratic media law—1962 Printers and Publishers Registration Law and Press Scrutiny and Registration Division (PSRD) needs a thorough overhauling for establishment of a more open and free mass-media regime in the country. In this background, this book has been divided into six chapters. The chapters look into the authoritarian political structure and try to investigate the character and operation of mass media in Myanmar.

The introductory chapter provides an overview of the book. It book into the main objectives and rationale of the book. It is followed by the research questions put up and the methodology adopted for its study. The chapter also reviews the main literatures available on the authoritarian regime in general and Myanmar in particular. It has also examined a number of literatures covering the functioning of mass media and freedom of speech and expression in Myanmar.

The second chapter provides a theoretical framework to the book. It has elaborated on the nature of authoritarian regimes with special reference to the case in Myanmar. The chapter also examines the socio-political roots of authoritarianism and Burmese political values. Under this background, this chapter elaborates the four theories of press as enumerated by Siebert et al. (1956), and applies the 'Authoritarian theory of Press' for studying the structure and functioning of mass media in Myanmar.

Chapter three is an overview of the post-colonial developments in Myanmar and beginning of militarization in the country. It also looks into the various phases of military rule beginning from 1962 by the revolutionary council followed by constitutional dictatorship under BSPP regime in 1974. It is followed by the direct military rule by the junta under the name of State Law and Order Restoration Council (SLORC) and finally the State Peace and Development Council (SPDC) from 1988. This chapter also provides an insight to the move made towards democratic transition and reconciliation in Myanmar.

Recent political developments are the main focus of chapter four. After five decades of authoritarian rule in Myanmar, the country faces a plethora of challenges both in the domestic and external affairs. In this background, this chapter studies the reform agenda of the new regime and the challenges of political transition in Myanmar.

Media in an authoritarian state is the main subject matter of chapter five. It discusses the evolution of mass media in

Myanmar with special focus on press censorship and restrictions during BSPP regime. This is followed by easing out of restrictions and emergence of private media houses during the period of liberalization in the 1990s. It also discusses the role of exiled media in Myanmar, which is considered as a blessing in disguise. The last section of this chapter discusses the new regime and media reforms in Myanmar.

The last chapter concludes the study with validation of the hypothesis. In the recent move towards democratic transition and national reconciliation, media in Myanmar is all set for reforms according to the international standards. Now all the major exiled media including the Mizzima, Democratic Voice of Burma and Irrawaddy have their presence in Yangon. An interim national press council was formed recently to prepare the new draft of media law. Journalists have already met and exchange views among themselves to determine desirable elements in the new media law. International and regional free media advocacy groups have poured into Myanmar to assist the journalists to increase their capacity, improve their professionalism and form professional organizations to protect press freedom.

Notes

1. Based on the report of Reporters Without Borders. http://en.rsf.org/press-freedom-index-2011-2012,1043.html
2. This was officially announced on 20 August 2012.
3. To change the press scrutiny policies step by step, 38 directives and 20 instructions issued under the 1962 Printers and Publishers Registration Law have been revoked, and only 13 directives and six instructions remain (as reported by *Myanmar Times,* August 27-September 2, 2012).
4. Based on personal interaction with journalists like Bertil Linter and Subhir Bhaumik.
5. Interaction with NLD MP (1990 elections) Dr. Tint Swe, Soe Myint, Thin Thin, Dr Aung Zaw Win, Nye Nye, Kim. Htun Htun, Dr. Khin Zaw Min, Myo Win, Dr. Aung Naing Oo, Aung Marm Oo, Ma Khin Ohmar, have deepened my understanding of Myanmar.
6. Insights from policymakers and diplomats like Amb. Shyam Saran, Amb Devere, Amb. Rajiv Bhatia have been really enriching.

Chapter 2

Theoretlcal Perspective: Media in an Authoritarian State

Authoritarianism is not peculiar only to Myanmar. It is prevalent throughout the world—in Africa, Latin America, East Asia, Middle East and in communist countries. But, in Southeast Asia, including Indonesia and Myanmar, authoritarianism was the way of life best known to the people of the region (Gyi 1983: v). It has been embedded in the Javanese concept of power and patrimonial authority in Indonesia (Anderson 1972) whereas in Myanmar it is a result of deep-seated belief in the Burmese political values with roots in Buddhist political and economic ideals (Steinberg 1982: 44). At the time of the withdrawal of the colonial rule, they established liberal parliamentary democracy in their respective countries. But they could not utilize the opportunities given by the liberal democratic framework and consequently within a few years of their gaining independence they reverted to authoritarianism either under civilian or military leadership (Sundhaussen 1995: 771).

Under this background, this chapter attempts to look at the fundamentals of authoritarianism in Myanmar. The first section of this chapter deals with the authoritarian model in Myanmar. In the second part, an attempt is made to study various theories of mass media and its application in the case of Myanmar. The key objective of this chapter is to reach a common understanding on the theoretical concept prior to establishing a framework for empirical assessment of mass media in an authoritarian state of Myanmar.

2.1 AUTHORITARIANISM

Authoritarianism denoting a particular rule pattern in human relationships is as old as mankind (Gyi 1983: 2). It is coeval with human society and persists to the present day. Authoritarianism is a system of relationships between state and society and between political and societal sources of power. It is based on a type of domination which is dependent on centralized executive control and coercion (Perlmutter 1981: 24). It is a belief and practice of government from above. Authoritarian regime emphasizes the claims of authority over those of individual liberty (Heywood 2002: 38). It is also a system that is designed to infiltrate the society and isolate it from the state, so that the latter has control over the former. Ideally, it is a system that makes a supreme effort to integrate the society into the mechanism of the state while giving the state the ultimate control (Perlmutter 1981: 24). It is in this context that Benedict Anderson (1983: 487) argues that the rise of New Order authoritarianism in Indonesia marks the resurrection of the state and its triumph vis-à-vis society and nation.

Authoritarian regimes are, by definition, not accountable or responsible in any direct, institutional fashion to the populace over whom they rule. But this does not mean that they exist in a vacuum, isolated from the population and not linked with it in any way. Every regime seeks to consolidate its position by embedding itself within the society (Gill 2000: 35). There is probably no country of any significant size where every single citizen regards the system of government as legitimate. Similarly, no regime, no matter how brutal and totalitarian, relies on force to survive (Diamond 2008a: 89). On the one hand, there are agents in the regime trying to apply force, on the other hand, there are factions having faith and belief in the system. Even if the majority detest the political system, as in Myanmar, there are always some regime loyalists who regard the regime as legitimate and who are devoted to its defence and maintenance.

Authoritarianism does not necessarily result in efficiency, achievement of the common good, political integration, modernization, or order, even if most modern authoritarian regimes strive to achieve some or all of these goals. The 'developmentalist authoritarian regimes' of East and Southeast Asia are good examples of this phenomenon (South Korea, Thailand, Indonesia, Singapore and Philippines). They often seek to justify the restrictive political frameworks as well as compensate for their political shortcomings by emphasizing economic development, security and stability often under the ideological garb of 'Asian values' (discussed in detail in the next section) (Alagappa 2001c: 471-72). But these have not been durable pillars of support. The experiences of these countries have shown that over the time, the gap between promise and delivery has widened, exposing the worthfulness of this development rhetoric and undermining the legitimacy of these governments. In this context, it must be understood that the projection of the image of technocratic governance of these regimes was only a part of the regime's strategy of containing internal as well as external criticism of its essentially authoritarian and predatory character (Hadiz 2004a: 58).

Authoritarian systems pay considerable energy to the formation and development of political structures (such as party, bureaucracy, police, armed forces, corporate organisations) that control the executive, penetrate the society, and, above all, promote elite cohesion (Case 2002: 24; Perlmutter 1981: 25). These political structures deal with the problems of both individual and societal mobilization, modernization, and social change. These structures of authoritarianism all compete for the attention of the authoritarian ruler.

At the outset, semantics clarity in between various terminologies associated with authoritarianism needs to be elaborated. These terminologies include: autocracy; tyranny; authoritarianism and totalitarianism. The conventional definition of autocracy, tyranny and authoritarianism are quite similar. Autocracy and tyranny describe the nature of the ruler while authoritarianism refers to the nature of the regime and the structure of its management. Autocracy may be defined as a rule by a single person wielding absolute executive power. Autocratic government contains no legal provision for limitation of powers, accountability, or orderly succession. Rule is arbitrary and maintained by force. Tyranny is virtually synonymous, being the arbitrary government instituted by law. Tyrannical authority is secured by conquest and maintained by fear (Perlmutter 1981: 1). An authoritarian regime may be a collective dictatorship, an oligarchy, or a military government. Although there has been a wide variety of authoritarian regimes historically (including one-party systems, military regimes, and personal dictatorships), they all tended to be deficient in key institutional features present in liberal democracies (Porter 2002: 8). Authoritarian systems lack responsive and accountable government, lack a transparent legal system, and tend to infringe citizens' liberties and rights. They commonly suffer from endemic corruption of the bureaucracy and are noted for enforcing 'limited pluralism', by denying legal scope to civil associations and parties, and restricting the participation and competition of citizens (Diamond 1990: 10-14). An ideal authoritarian system does not tolerate cleavages, opposition, political pluralism, or even limited freedom of ideas. Although in some cases (as in Indonesia and Myanmar), it does not deny constitutional authority, yet the rule of law and functional representation are modified by the absolute priority placed on order and stability.

A totalitarian state attempts to control nearly every aspect of personal, economic and political life of its citizens.[1] The concept of totalitarianism emerged in the 1920s and 1930s as a part of the ideology of Fascist Italy (Brooker 2000: 8). Benito Mussolini was the first to use the word totalitarian to describe his dictatorship positively. In 1950s, totalitarianism re-emerged as a prominent concept in Western political science in the classic work of Hannah Arendt, Fredrich, Brzezinski and Schapiro (Momayezi 2006: 1555-58). The totalitarian state rests on unlimited, unconstitutional state power and leads to the "enlargement of the public or political sphere so as to include even private life and morality within the reach of political action" (Goodwin 2007: 179). It prohibits all activities which are contrary to the regime's goals. According to Juan Linz, "the dimensions that we have to retain as necessary to characterize a system as totalitarian are: an ideology; a single mass party and other mobilisational organization; and concentrated power in an individual or a small group that is not accountable to the public and which cannot be dislodged from power by institutionalized and peaceful means" (Linz 2000: 67). Each of these elements can be found separately in other types of non-democratic systems and only their simultaneous presence makes a system totalitarian (*ibid.*).

Totalitarianism also means coercion of the centrality of the political power and the emergence of political elite, a "totalitarian class" for whom totalitarianism is also a workable ideal. The function of totalitarianism is revolutionary, that is, the politicization of society (Perlmutter 1981: 65). The main examples of regimes considered totalitarian are Nazi Germany, Fascist Italy, Bolshevism under Lenin and Stalin, Baathist Iraq, Communist China under Mao, and Cambodia under Khmer Rouge. The most powerful means of control is the ideology, the instrument of persuasion and indoctrination (Goodwin 2007: 179).

Authoritarian is distinguished from totalitarian both in degree and scope (Heywood 2002: 38). Authoritarian administration is less intrusive and not necessarily backed by the use of force. Typically, the government in an authoritarian regime is run by an elite group that uses repressive means to stay in power such as monarchical absolutism, traditional dictatorships and military rule. However, unlike totalitarian regimes, there is no desire or ideological justification for the state to control all aspects of a person's life. They tolerate a significant range of economic, religious and other freedoms. Totalitarian governments tend to be revolutionary and intend to change the basic structure of society, authoritarian ones tend to be conservative.

The totalitarian school argues that the ideology (messianic, racist, anti-Semitic) is an organic, and the most conspicuous, component of mass authoritarianism. It may be successfully demonstrated that the three most notorious authoritarian ideological movements in modern times—Bolshevism, Fascism and Nazism—were the primary or necessary political vehicles for the establishment of the authoritarian regimes that supported them (Perlmutter 1981: 62). The reason why ideology is considered to be so important is that it becomes an instrument of maintenance in power of the party controlling it. Propaganda and educational training are viewed as the means for achieving total ideological integration of the people (Momayezi 2006: 1558). Thus, Mussolini, Hitler, Lenin and Stalin confidently believed in totalitarian solutions and in the ultimate success of totalitarian systems.

The concept has been revived in 1970s by a political sociologist Juan J. Linz in his comparative study "Totalitarian and Authoritarian Regimes". An authoritarian regime is totalitarian if it has the following attributes (Linz 1975: 175):

(a) a monistic but not monolithic centre of power;
(b) an exclusive, autonomous, and more or less intellectually elaborate ideology that serves to legitimize the leaders power;
(c) citizen's participation and active mobilization for political and collective social tasks.

Linz's version of totalitarianism is distinguished from authoritarian systems by the use of ideology as an instrument of legitimation. Totalitarian systems possess an exclusive ideology while authoritarian systems lack an "elaborate and guiding ideology, with distinctive mentalities" (*ibid.*: 264). In its transition from authoritarianism to totalitarianism, Linz identifies a 'grey zone' between both under different nomenclatures—quasi-totalitarianism, post-totalitarianism, rationalized totalitarianism, totalitarianism without terror (Linz 2000: 240-52).

2.1.1 Authoritarian Regimes

Political thinkers use the term authoritarian regimes rather than authoritarian government to indicate the relatively low specificity of political institutions. They often penetrate the life of the society, preventing even forcibily, the political expression of certain group interests (as religion in Turkey, labour in Spain) or shaping them by interventionist policies like those of corporatist regime (in Indonesia) (Linz 2000: 160). There is a clear distinction between modern and early notions of authoritarianism. The early version was the rule by the few in the name of the many (Perlmutter 1981: 2). Modern authoritarianism is further distinguished by limited political pluralism, without elaborate and guiding ideology and without an extensive or intensive form of political mobilization, except at some points in their development. The leader or a small group in an authoritarian regime, exercises power within formally ill-defined limits (Linz 2000: 159). The regime may, however, be limited, exclusionary, and restrictive, but above all based on specialized political structures and institutions (Perlmutter 1981: 2).

The major purpose of modern authoritarian regime is to establish the political elites' domination over society by arresting subverting or destroying autonomous individual collective and institutional behaviour and thus, to enhance the power of authorities at the expense of autonomy (Perlmutter 1981: 24). Though the authoritarian regime tries to destroy disorderly and potentially anti-authoritarian forms of group behaviour, it is dedicated to integrating other citizens and interest groups, political parties and social movements into the state. It does this by infiltrating and subverting these groups and inducing them to become the part of the newly formed organizations aimed at political mobilization. In other words, authoritarian regimes attempt to co-opt, subdue or eliminate all sources of political power outside the state system, whether they are mass based or controlled by social elites (Linz 2000: 167).

There are three major instruments for the intervention, penetration, and supervision of collective and institutional behaviour whose functions are delineated, but integrative (Perlmutter, 1981: 10-11) (Fig. 2.1):

(i) the single authoritarian party;

(ii) the bureaucratic military complex—State;

(iii) Parallel and auxiliary structures of domination, mobilization and control such as police or paramilitary forces.

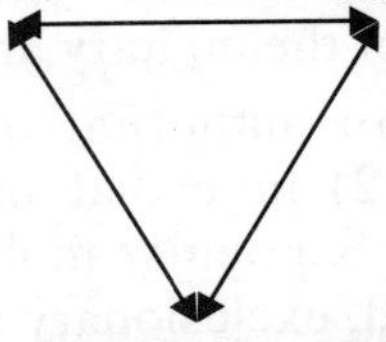

Fig. 2.1: Instruments for Intervention in Authoritarian Regimes.

Source: Perlmutter, Amos (1981), *Modern Authoritarianism*, New Haven, Conn.: Yale University Press, p. 10.

These instruments are employed differently by different types of authoritarian regimes. Each type of authoritarian regime, while employing all three, will favour one instrument over the others. One regime may dispense with the use of the single party and employ the military as the instrument of domination. Another type would make extensive use of the political police at the expense of the single party and the military. Similarly, others might enhance the patrimonial-clientalist and corporatist groups, at the expense of party and the state. Still another might use revolutionary guards—an auxiliary instrument—to replace the party.

The notion of 'authoritarian regime' is often used as a synonym for 'non-democratic regimes'. They focus on a particular regime type—military rule, one-party rule or personalistic dictatorship (Brooker 2000: 36). The type of authoritarianism is determined by the roles of three political instruments (mentioned above) of authoritarianism; actual and relative political influence wielded by these political instruments; the preferential use of these instruments by the authoritarian regimes; the dynamics of authoritarian rule and in the long run the relative influence of the political structures of authoritarian systems (Perlmutter 1981: 24). Accordingly, the different types of authoritarian regimes are distinguished by the ways these instruments are employed. The relationship among the three produces different types of authoritarian political behaviour. Since all authoritarian regimes compete for political support, authoritarian systems are also differentiated according to priority each instrument is given. The hard authoritarian model of Myanmar relies on the personalistic and autocratic tyranny of the military and the propaganda.

In discussing modern authoritarianism Linz (2000: 165) and Perlmutter (1981: 2) note that one of the things upon which such regimes rest is popular mobilization. But this kind of mobilization is limited, exclusionary and restrictive. A range of bodies may be generated to organize and structure public activity including youth groups, trade unions women groups, sporting associations, etc. The aim of such organisation is to keep the people busy and to involve them in an activity which is essentially regime is supporting (Gill 2000: 13). The crucial element here is to ensure that such public activity is controlled, and to ensure that there is no popular mobilization on an independent basis. This leads to the destruction and continuing suppression of all types of independent organization, especially those which have greater potential. The industrial, business and the technocratic elites that emerge out of the corporatist model acts as a social support base for many conservative authoritarianism. These groups often see the 'state' as a source of substantial material support for their economic activities (*ibid.*: 15). If 'rupture' arises in this ruling class elite base, then the likely chances of transformation and transition become stronger (Diamond 2008a: 90). In many cases, according to Wood (2004: 107), authoritarian regimes actually laid the institutional foundations for the subsequent rise of democracy.

Historically, non-authoritarian regimes may take a variety of sub-forms: absolute monarchies, feudal aristocracies, fascist states, personalistic or autocratic military regimes. But according to Huntington (1991: 110), the regimes that moved towards democracy in the third wave generally fall into three groups—one-party system, military regimes and personal dictatorships. Others like Pinkney (2004: 159-60), O'Niel (2006), Mc Cormick (1995: 335-36) have also adhered to this typology of authoritarian regimes. Perlmutter (1981: 130) adds one more category to it, viz. corporatist.

Existence of a single or privileged party is an important component of authoritarian regimes (Linz 2000: 161). Often such parties are creation from above rather than from the grassroots—created by groups in power. In these systems, the party effectively monopolizes power, access to power is through the party organization, and the party legitimizes its rule through ideology. According to Huntington (1991: 110), these systems often achieved a relatively high level of political institutionalization. It also poses ideological barriers to democratization (Pinkney 2004: 161).

In a personalistic-autocratic framework, power remains personalized and centralized and is often based around a cult of personality. Weber's typology of personalistic dictatorship in his notions of 'charismatic' and 'traditional-patrimonial rule' have become two of the best known terms used in the study of non-democratic regimes. He has pointed to how the impersonal nature of the 'legal-rational' type of legitimate rule contrasted with the personalist nature of the other two types (quoted in Brooker 2000: 52). The ruler is often the pivot of state power and the government rises and falls with the fortunes of the leader (Mc Cormick 1995: 336). The distinguishing characteristic of a personal dictatorship is that the individual leader is the source of authority and that "power depends upon access to, closeness to, dependence on and support from the leader" (Huntington 1991: 111). The absence of effective political institutions results in the predominance of a personal authority and power that is limited more by countervailing forces than by institutions. Personal rule is a system of personal relations centred on the rulers' relations with his associates, clients, supporters and rivals (Brooker 2000: 57). Such personal rule is also inherently authoritarian in its monopolizing of power and it can arise in military as well as party regimes. In most cases, it may take the form of military authoritarianism.

The military regimes are created by coup d'etat replacing democratic or civilian governments. The military exercises power on an institutional basis, with the military leaders typically either governing collegially as junta (in Myanmar) or circulating the top governmental position among top generals (in Indonesia) (Huntington 1991: 110). S.E. Finer (1962) in his classic work *Man on Horseback: The Role of the Military in Politics* identifies five different forms of military regime: two direct, two indirect and one dual (quoted in Brooker 2000: 44). The first and the standard model is of 'direct rule' which involves openly military rule by a military junta with leading military officers installed as the country's head and ministers. Myanmar's military junta is one of the existing manifestations of this regime type. According to Soe Mynt, "We do not find a full-fledged government, but rather a group of military official actually controls the entire governmental machinery and rule the country through direct brute force".[2] Ne Win's 'Revolutionary Council' and the SLORC/SPDC regimes illustrate this model (Silverstein 1977; Steinberg 1981; Fink 2001; Callahan 2001). It is a form of simple military tyranny. The second typology of direct military rule is 'quasi civilianized in form'. Its civilian form may include a supportive political party and even the electoral process. But all these are a façade, emanating from and dependent on the military. Indonesia under Suharto is an explicit model of this regime type. The Golkar, bureaucractic and corporatist nexus appropriated the state power for itself (Hadiz 2004b: 616). Moreover, series of elections held regularly since 1971 by Suharto's New Order military regime was an attempt to justify its highly authoritarian and centralized character (Anderson 1998: 282). Finer's 'dual type' of military regime involves organized civilian support developed by a military dictator that can act as a counterpoise to the views and influence of the army. As the head of both the military and this civilian organization, he can strengthen his personal position by establishing a balance of power between the dual, military and civilian bases of the regime (quoted in Brooker 2000: 45). Finer has also identified two types of indirect military regimes. The 'indirect-limited' type sees the military exerting control over the government only intermittently. In contrast, the 'indirect-complete' type sees the military continuously controlling all the activities of the civilian government.

Military intervention and domination occurred in countries where the legitimacy of the nation state and the system of political domination was weak and contested, and where civilian leaders relied on state coercion to sustain their power (Alagappa 2001c: 470). In these countries, the power and the influence of the military increased, usually to the detriment of civilian leaders and institution. The regime relies heavily on military as a tool of state power, so losing the support of the military almost inevitably leads to a loss of political power (Mc Cormick 1995: 338).

Perlmutter has identified another type of military regime—the corporatist model—where the government is the most powerful patron. The state performs managerial, bureaucratic, technocratic functions and is both repressive and efficient. Government is composed of military and technocratic groups and it dominates the corporatist social systems (Perlmutter 1981: 42). This has been exemplified in the rise of powerful politico-capitalist families with rapacious, predatory interests in Indonesia (Hadiz 2004b: 616). The protagonists of Indonesian development process have invariably been economic technocrats and other intellectuals, mostly schooled in neo-classical tradition who struggled to enforce 'rational policy' in the face of an intrusive patrimonial style of politics (Hadiz 2004a: 59). The regime relies on the state bureaucracy and the military for support. The Indonesian model is an example of how an authoritarian government has used corporatist methods to maintain stability and growth during Suharto's rule (Porter 2002: 24-33).

Corporatism is a political system in which organizations officially represent private interest and the range of state activities is wide. In its broadest sense, it is a means of incorporating organized interests into the processes of government. Long associated with the fascist regimes of the inter-war period, the concept of corporatism has been rehabilitated within political analysis in 1970s and is widely applied in studies of organized interests in democratic as well as authoritarian settings (Cawson 1991: 106). According to Andrew Heywood (2002: 275), there are two faces of corporatism. First, authoritarian corporatism is an ideology charecterised by political intimidation of industry and the destruction of the independent trade unions. Schmitter (1974: 85-131) calls it as 'state corporatism'. It tends to be associated with peripheral or dependent capitalist regimes such as those in Latin America (Malloy 1977; Collier 1995). It has also been used in Indonesian political discourse (Mc Intyre 1994; Ghosh 1996; Porter 2002). Second, liberal corporatism is found in mature liberal democracies for organized interests to be granted privileged and institutional access to policy formulation (Heywood 2002: 275). In contrast with its authoritarian variant, liberal corporatism strengthens groups in relation to government, not the other way round. Also called as 'societal corporatism', it has become most strongly institutionalized in countries such as Austria or Sweden where a powerful labour movement has become a social partner with the state in negotiating economic and social policies (Cawson 1991: 104).

Focusing on corporatist arrangements in an authoritarian context, Alfred Stepan differentiates between two sub-types: exclusionary and inclusionary corporatism (quoted in Mc Intyre 1994: 2). Although neither is democratic, as the labels suggest, the first is characterised by greater control and repression, whereas under the second, although the state is still unquestionably dominant, there is much greater scope for societal input through approved interest associations. As will become clear, in the case of New Order Indonesia, corporatist institutions have for the most part been decidedly exclusionary in nature.

In a corporatist regime, additional source of political support is the military establishment (Perlmutter 1981: 130-32). A corporate military regime restricts political support and mobilization, except for those coming from the military establishment. The corporate regime seeks additional political support outside of the military among the different state-linked corporate groups. It is sincere in calling elections, even if the choice is limited to an executive chosen by the military. This type of regime might tolerate national political institutions and structure such as Parliament, parties and pressure groups. It also tolerates local governments and other authorities that are not directly dominated or directed by the military. Political bargaining is conducted between organized groups. The military either arbitrates or dictates policies.

According to Andreas Schedler (2006), "under electoral authoritarian rule, elections are broadly inclusive (they are held under universal suffrage) as well as minimally pluralistic (opposition parties are allowed to run), minimally competitive (opposition parties, while denied victory, are allowed to win votes and seats), and minimally open (opposition parties are not subject to massive repression, although they may experience repressive treatment in selective and intermittent ways)" (p. 3). The electoral contests are severely manipulated by the state and there is hardly any scope for electoral democracy. This when studied in the wake of the 2010 elections in Myanmar could be easily validated. Although the election was supposed to be inclusive, yet it debarred a large section of people from voting. Elections were cancelled in several violence-hit regions inhabited by ethnic nationalities. This had disenfranchised a large section of the population from participation in the country's largest democratic exercise in the last 20 years (*Jakara Times* 2010; TNI 2010). Opposition has claimed of widespread electoral irregularities, including intimidation of voters by the government. There were serious allegations with regard to the actual vote count, particularly in relation to the advance vote (Turnell 2011; TNI 2010; ICG 2011a). Advance votes were collected with allegations of serious irregularities. Election laws were in itself discriminatory. Out of 37 parties which were registered only, 23 parties participated in the election. The largest opposition party, NLD was forced to disband, but however one of its splinter group NDF participated. In the absence of any major opposition, the government-backed USDP was able to back around 80 per cent of the seats in the Parliament. Heavy restrictions were also imposed on the media coverage and no foreign observers were allowed inside the country. Several restrictions were imposed on campaign speech and media airtime. Thus, the manner in which the elections were conducted depicts Myanmar's transition not to a full-fledged civilian democracy, rather a move towards electoral authoritarianism. According to Schedler (2006), "Authoritarian manipulation may come under many guises, all serving the purpose of containing the troubling uncertainty of electoral outcomes. Rulers may devise discriminatory electoral rules, exclude opposition parties and candidates from entering the electoral arena, infringe upon their political rights and civil liberties, restrict their access to mass media and campaign finance, impose formal or informal suffrage restrictions on their supporters, coerce or corrupt them into deserting the opposition camp, or simply redistribute votes and seats through electoral fraud".

2.1.2 Authoritarianism in Myanmar

Military authoritarian rule with command economy and restricted freedom imposed by General Ne Win and his coterie of military officers in Myanmar is expression of an autocratic military framework in Myanmar (Silverstein 1977; Steinberg 1981; Gyi 1983; Alamgir 1997; Callahan 2001; Fink 2001). Myanmar since 1962 has been ruled by military known in Myanmar as the *Tatmadaw*. In the leadership vacuum created in 1962, Ne Win seized power and established a 'Revolutionary Council' to govern the state (Alamgir 1997: 438). He subsequently banned all political parties and dissent and organized Myanmar as a one-party state under the Burma Socialist Programme Party (BSPP). The elimination of political parties and the severe restrictions on civil liberties and freedoms marked the expansion of authoritarian rule (Silverstein 1977: 100). BSPP, which was established in 1962, was a cadre organization of military elite for its first nine years and was finally converted into a mass organization in 1971 (Steinberg 1981: 31). Ne Win ruled until 1988. Ne Win resigned in July 1988 as thousands of students were killed in military firings on demonstrations between March and September. General Saw Maung took over as the new ruler of Myanmar (Callahan 2001: 424). One-party authoritarianism under BSPP rule was abrogated and military authoritarianism was established under the SLORC junta which was renamed as SPDC in 1997 to create a softer image of the ruthless military authoritarianism (Fink 2001: 94). In an effort to control public opinion, political opposition has been systematically intimidated and all media have been censored (Callahan 2001: 424).

Maung Maung Gyi (1983) has studied the Burmese political values as they evolved over the centuries from the monarchical days to modern times. The Burmese monarchy is distinguished by three features: the sacro-sanctity and the central position of the kingship; absolutism of the Burmese Monarchy; and undifferentiated function of kingship. The king was responsible to himself alone (Gyi 1983: 23). The king was not only the chief executive but also the chief judge and the chief legislator of the land. As shown above, there was not only lack of limitation of king's power, but also lack of differentiation of his powers. In this context, the imposition of the authoritarian regime by military elite dominated by one man, General Ne Win exemplifies a rule pattern not unlike those of monarchical days. Perhaps, Ne Win is not entirely to be blamed for the military coup nor the resultant political system. In fact, military coup may be conceived of as the culmination of a political process. The government was entirely dominated by the political cliques and their power mad leaders engaged mostly in factional fights and it was tempting for a well-organised institution such as the military to intervene and impose its authoritarian rule (Gyi 1983: 3). The right soil for the growth of an authoritarian system reminiscent of native Burmese monarchical rule was already there in the society.[3] Pre-conditions for the retreat to native authoritarian rule patterns were lying dormant in the minds of the majority of the Burmese public. Ne Win's authoritarian political style merely cashed in on this vast store of built in attitudes and values of the Burmese society that are supportive of his rule pattern. Thus, authoritarianism in lines with the old Burmese values returned and has stayed in Myanmar since last 45 years.

After the coup, General Ne Win and his Revolutionary Council (RC) immediately set about imposing order, and the universities were one of the first targets. The military regime announced stricter regulations for university students (Fink 2001: 31). The regime tried to stamp out resistance by increasing surveillance and limiting contact between students. Through his RC, General Ne Win sought to remake Burmese politics and society. The RC developed policies that were a product of shared military tradition, common nationalistic aspirations and socialist thought (Steinberg 1981: 27). Land and wealth were to be redistributed, foreigner stripped of their assets and self-serving politicians and capitalists replaced with loyal army dedicated to serving the nation. The RC instituted what was called 'The Burmese Way to Socialism'. Between 1963 and 1965, all banks, industries and large shops were nationalized. Most of the businesses were run by Indians and Chinese, by taking state control, the government intended to return profits to the indigenous Burmese. In March 1964, the RC demonetized 50 kyat and 100 kyat notes also with the intention of removing wealth from the foreign hands (Silverstein 1977: 155-57). As a result, hundreds of thousands of Indians and Chinese business people lost everything and left the country. Those businesses that did not collapse came under state ownership (Fink 2001: 32).

As the RC expanded its control, most independent associations were either absorbed by the government or forced out of existence. All publications had to pass through a newly formed censorship Board. Private schools were nationalized and a government-controlled Burmese language curriculum was imposed throughout the country. Meanwhile, most foreign missionaries, scholars and Western foundations were forced to leave and foreigner's access to Myanmar was tightly restricted. Independent trade unions were outlawed and existing political parties were also compelled to disband, with the only legal political party being the governments' Burma Socialist Programme Party (BSPP) (Steinberg 1981: 31). Originally, membership in the BSPP was restricted to the military and the administration, however, the regime later expanded membership and established other mass organizations under state control.

With the development of one party system, General Ne Win sought to use the BSPP to cement the allegiance of the civil servants and others to his military backed regime. In the 1970s, party membership was open to all and not joining carried negative consequences. Party officers took over many of the administrative posts at all levels of government and civil servants were expected to become members (Steinberg 1981: 31; Silverstein 1977: 100). The judicial system also offered little hope of a fair hearing. Under the RC, courts were run by a panel of three judges, at least one of whom had to have some legal training. During the BSPP period, the three judges were elected but had to be party members. The chairman of the three judges was generally a military officer, while the other two judges came from the people and frequently included individuals with little education. From the government perspective, a lack of education was not a problem because 'goodness' mainly characterised by loyalty was more important (Fink 2001: 39).

All associations were controlled by members of the ruling junta; the wives of the generals often lead civic organizations. There were only a few grassroots organizations with very limited mobility. Civil groups or associations were co-opted by the military and there was hardly any room to maneuver independent of the military (Alagappa 2001c: 494). Despite market reforms, since the end of the 1980s, large state enterprises have dominated key economic sectors such as energy and heavy industry. These state enterprises enjoyed competitive advantages and the special protection of the ruling military elite because of their loyalty to the existing regime. There was no state policy on competition and development except some commonly recognized rules. State banks were controlled by the military leaders and they enjoyed special privileges which was not granted to the country's private banks. They were not allowed to conduct business with foreign clients. Foreign trade was essentially limited to the export of natural gas and agricultural products. The government consistently suppressed opposition activities, used extra-judicial killings, disappearances, torture, arbitrary arrests, denial of fair trial rights and more. In addition to restrictions of human rights and freedoms, other factors also contributed to a silent emergency in Myanmar (Sarkin and Pietschmann 2003). Poverty, hunger, disease, sexual violence and insurgency are few of them.

The military has dominated the political and social system for the last 40 years. The last free elections took place in 1990, but the military junta refused to recognize the results (Thawnghmung 2003: 457; Smith 1999: 23). The military government was not elected by the people but rather took power in a *coup d'etat*. It completely controlled all domestic media and blocked independent reporting by foreign journalists. The entire population was denied essential aspects of full citizenship and crippled in its political expression. The country's largest opposition party, the National League for Democracy (NLD) continues to suffer extreme repressive measures. Its leadership is being kept under house arrest and members are under permanent surveillance by the secret police. Thus, the autocratic rule of Ne Win provided a framework for the military junta to thrive in later years.

2.1.3 Political Culture and Values

The rule pattern of a government is reflective of the prevailing political culture which is not an overnight creation. It is organic in nature and grows over years absorbing mainly the political experience of the people and the role they are expected to play in the political order vis-à-vis the ruling elite of the country (Gyi 1983: 7). Furthermore, political traditions and folklores, political myths and symbols, social values and customs and religious teachings pertinent to the political system are all interwoven into this complex network of political and social structure. Hence, it is relevant to explore the traditional Burmese values and belief system that underwent little change during the British colonial rule. Many of the traditional values and attitudes that characterised pre-colonial Myanmar persisted through the period of foreign rule, and continued even after independence (Silverstein 1977: 35).

The authority of the Burmese king was neither distinguished nor circumscribed. The king was the central figure in the old Burmese system of government. He was the pivot around which the wheel of administration revolved. He was the core of whole nation and his palace was referred to as 'the centre of the universe'. He was the embodiment of the highest attainment on earth, and according to Buddhist philosophy, "kingship was a position earned through merits accumulated in the numberless cycle of existence in the past and, therefore, not easily to be achieved. The king claimed to be lineal descendant of *Mahathamada*" (the first king of the world also known as 'Manu') (Gyi 1983: 14). His conscience alone controlled his actions and thus, ultimately, it came to mean that it was the personality of the king that largely determined the character of the government. (*ibid.*: 34). The actual concentration of powers in one person and the manner in which these powers had been exercised led the people to believe that the king and his agents were capable of exercising "any and every function whatsoever" (*ibid.*: 35).

Authoritarian nature of the traditional Burmese state was based on highly personalized concepts of power and central authority. These stem back to the system of semi-divine rule which has sustained it (Carey 1997: 3). From 1044 to 1885, for over 800 years, the Burmese lived under absolute monarchy. Its authority was never challenged by any liberal forces during these years until it was overthrown by an alien power in 1885 (Gyi 1983: 13-14). Burmese thought pattern towards the government was molded during this 800 years and the nature of kingship largely determined the pattern of thought. Although the colonial period effectively destroyed this monarchical tradition in Myanmar, the centralising processes of the late Burman monarchy were carried on under the British (1826-1948)[4] (Carey 1997: 3).

Authoritarianism emerged as the core value in this evolutionary process. Burmese have traditionally identified the government as one of the five elements—others being fire, water (floods and storms), thieves and malevolent people. Ordinary people had never had much control over the political process and felt it was just best to get on with life regardless of who was in power (Fink 2001: 29-30). Although the government did seek to develop the country, there was little substantive dialogue between politicians and the people in their constituencies. As a result, democracy was only superficially rooted in Myanmar, and the military was able to take over with little resistance. Burmese reverted to the traditional political system of authoritarian rule, on March 2, 1962, when General Ne Win put an end to the parliamentary system with plurality of parties and free elections (Gyi 1983: 7). Most of the patrimonial elements and the patron client relations that dominated the functioning of the parliamentary democracy continued to persist under the two subsequent regimes. It was precisely due to this persistence of patrimonial nature of the state throughout the post-independence period that authoritarianism has continued to dominate in Myanmar (Hlaing 2008: 176).

The rejection of the British parliamentary democracy with all its strengths and weaknesses attests to the fact that the alien political institution and values have failed to strike roots in Myanmar. The experience of Parliamentary democracy under U Nu often represented his deeply Burmese religious and cultural sensibilities with the country's politics. Although the state was officially secular, U Nu was establishing himself as the patron of Buddhism in the same way that Burmese king had in the past (Fink 2001: 26). Military elites infused with traditional values, led the Burmese people and went back to their age-old political habits and rule pattern reminiscent of their semi-feudal, autocratic government headed by a king as a real head and mainspring of the whole governmental system. The Burmese continue to accept authority from above and have never widely accepted the idea of authority stemming from the people (Silverstein 1977: 35). Thus, Buddhist values and attitudes are still the major influences on Burmese thought.

From the very outset, the coup leaders never seemed to doubt the legitimacy of their actions (Silverstein 1977: 80). Their publications and speeches demonstrated their belief in the right of the military to intervene and alter the government in the time of national crisis. In order to unite with the people and inform them where and how the military intended to lead the revolution, the coup leaders wrote a new ideology that would become their blueprint. This ideology is contained in two documents—"Burmese Way to Socialism" (BWS) and "System of Correlation of Man and His Environment" (SCME) (Steinberg 1981: 28; 1982: 41-44; Alamgir 1997: 340; Silverstein 1977: 80-85). They represented a new stage in the development and formulation of military's concept of a national ideology.

"Burmese Way to Socialism" gave a direction to the Burmese authoritarianism. This model of Socialism was compatible with the traditional Burmese values and Buddhist traditions (Alamgir 1997: 340). In Myanmar, there was a re-interpretation of the Buddhist political and economic ideals—a Buddhist welfare state—and an equating of that ideals with contemporary Burmese nationalist and social needs (Steinberg 1982: 44). This dynamic inter-play of Buddhism and Socialism, in the Burmese context, has been continuous since 1930s (discussed in detail in Chapter 3). Socialism in Myanmar, was thus, fully harmonised with the religious beliefs and cultural background and heritage of the people (Silverstein 1977: 87). The Revolutionary Council also published an ideological proclamation entitled *The System of Correlation of Man and His Environment* which tried to blend the Marxist notion of dialectics with Buddhist theological concepts about change (Alamgir 1977: 340). "The Burmese beliefs were not based on the theory of inevitable progress—but on the idea of change as a constant in all material and non-material things, and men and society should progress or regress dependency on their own ideas and endeavours" (Silverstein 1977: 86). This interplay between Buddhism and Socialism in that period was so complete that there was an association of Marxist monks within the Buddhist Sangha (Steinberg 1982: 44).

The authoritarian element was not confined to the political domain. It had its parallel in the social sphere as well. The Burmese social system was conceived in terms of ordered relationship based on moral obligations. The system, thus, established was highly personalized hierarchical system which guided the relationships between the superior and the inferior and older person and a younger person and a person of higher status and a person of lower status. Each was morally bound to fulfill his or her obligation or duties. It was based on will guided by morals rather than an individual system based on positive law. Popular participation in the governance of the country had never been a native concept (Gyi 1983: 39). The ministers were not the people's representative but the king's officers and they enjoyed office during his pleasure. The king and his bureaucracy of courtiers and officials took upon themselves the task of deciding what was best for the people and the country (*ibid.*: 40).

The aforesaid mentioned features of Burmese monarchy along with actual administrative practices such as arbitrary actions, monopoly of power, and use of violence and terror in forcing compliance with royal commands have generated in the minds of ordinary laymen a general attitude of helplessness and resignation against the government that many came to view as omnipotent and omnipresent. Many Burmese saying attest to this conclusion, for example, (*bayen do phone mou thou chone lu pone taw mha ma nay thah*), i.e. the authority of the monarch is like a thunder clap, criminals hiding in the jungle must surrender because they could not stand its terrifying sound and (*min nar ta htaung min myaung ta thein*) a king has 1,000 ears and 1,00,000 royal messengers (Gyi 1983: 48). Furthermore, superstition of the courts; its arrogance and pride; and its inefficiency largely reflected an undeveloped and primitive type of administration as well as the political immaturity and gullibility of the Burmese people of those days. These governmental and the national traits persist in varying degrees to this day as well.

2.2 THEORETICAL PARADIGM

Each country's mass media system is determined by its political philosophy. These controlling philosophies have even started since then without people noticing or knowing it. From the earliest civilizations up to now, various controlling philosophies are playing a great role in a certain nation's political and even mass media system. Based on an analysis of authority structures and institutions of political architecture in

Myanmar, the mass media can at best be characterised as having based on authoritarian theory. Following section gives a description of the four theories of mass media and communication and the relevance of authoritarian theory in the case of Myanmar.

The earliest theories were those propounded by Western theorists Siebert, Paterson and Schramm in their book *Four Theories of the Press* (1956). These were termed "normative theories" in the sense that they "mainly express ideas of how the media ought to or can be expected to operate under a prevailing set of conditions and values." Each of the four original or classical theories is based on a particular political theory or economic scenario. The four theories which have determined what kind of press the Western world has had. The authoritarian theory grounded in centuries of authoritarian political thought from Plato to Machiavelli; the libertarian grounded in Milton, Locke, Mill and the Enlightenment; the social responsibility grounded in a communication revolution and in certain behaviouristic doubts about philosophy of the Enlightenment and the Soviet Communist, ground in Marx, Lenin, Stalin and the dictatorship of the Communist Party in the Soviet Union (*ibid.*).

2.2.1 Authoritarian Theory

Authoritarian doctrine has determined the mass communication pattern for more people over a longer period of time than any other theory. This theory stemmed from the authoritarian philosophy of Plato (407-327 B.C), who thought that the state was safe only in the hands of a few wise men. Thomas Hobbes (1588-1679) argued that the power to maintain order was sovereign and individual objections were to be ignored. Engel, a German thinker further reinforced the theory by stating that freedom came into its supreme right only under Authoritarianism.

What Fred S. Siebert said:

> For almost two hundred years after the spread of printing in the western world, the authoritarian theory furnished

> the exclusive basis for determining the function and relationship of the popular press to contemporary society.
>
> ...in fact practically all western Europe...utilized the basic principles of authoritarianism as the theoretical foundation for their systems of press control.

The world has been witness to authoritarian means of control over media by both dictatorial and democratic governments. Ownership of printing remains mostly in private hands, but broadcasting and cinema usually remain in the hands of government. The form of control the government exercises over media in authoritarian countries is the same as the control it has over the people who live there. The concepts are inseparable. That is, one follows the other. Throughout history, authoritarian regimes such as Germany under Hitler and Italy under Mussolini have used propaganda. It's shading the news and information to fit a preconceived conclusion on what the information should mean and on how people should interpret it. (*Four Theories of the Press*, 9).

> **From Mein Kampf (my struggle):**
>
> All propaganda should be popular and should adapt its intellectual level to the receptive ability of the least intellectual of those whom it is desired to address.
>
> This was one of the ways Hitler was able to control the people. (*Four Theories of the Press*, p. 16)

The authoritarian concept is the oldest and most pervasive of all the theories. In this concept, the press is always subject to direct or implied control by the state or sovereign. In the traditional sense, the press operates outside of the government and is allowed to gather and publish news but it must function for "the good of the state." The press functions from the top down in these systems—the regime declares what is newsworthy because truth and information are a monopoly of those in power. Diversity of views is considered wasteful and dissent is annoying. It is also possible for democratic nations to have an authoritarian press under certain conditions such as war or terrorist attacks.

This approach is practiced wherever an authoritarian government is in place. Obviously, all shades of authoritarianism exist. The most significant examples are Libya, Syria, Zimbabwe, Mynamar, Belarus and Uzbekistan. Myanmar, quashed the pro-democracy movement and detained its leader, Aung San Suu Ky. Formerly, authoritarian control existed in the Philippines under Ferdinand Marcos and in South Korea, Nicaragua, Iraq and South Africa under apartheid. The authoritarian government can be secular or religious. In recent times, many governments have become more authoritarian as a result of religious influences. Iran is the best example of that. And so was Afganistan under the Taliban. Many governments are entirely secular, yet extremely authoritarian. The best example of that is Myanmar. Still, some countries are considered authoritarian with additional information required to put everything into context. Saudi Arabia has become more rigid, mostly because of religious influence. Singapore is totally secular but still tightly controlled in many ways.

Just as access to alternative sources of information is an essential feature of democracy, misinformation and disinformation, according to Schedler (2010: 74) constitute core features of authoritarianism. To minimize citizens' exposure to competing constructions of political reality, non-democratic rulers can place restrictions on means of communication, media content and media consumption (*ibid.*):

—to restrict private control over means of production and distribution of political information, authoritarian regimes typically exercise state monopolies of print, broadcast, or electronic media. Some dictatorial states have even gone further of denying operating licenses or public advertising, or by having the police, tax administration, or anti-corruption bureau shutting down. There is hardly any scope for private media to operate under such constraints.

—authoritarian states that leave means of communication in private hands often turn to restricting media content. Sometimes, they use censorship regulations. At other times, they resort to more informal, indirect techniques, such as beating up journalists. Both legal censorship and extralegal intimidation tend to induce self censorship.

—to restrict the consumption of available information by citizens, rulers may legally prohibit or materially disable mass access to information that has been produced outside the bounds of authoritarian control including international media, blogs and various social networking cites.

2.2.2 The Soviet-Communist Theory

It is related to the authoritarian theory. The main difference is that under the Soviet-Communist system, the state owns or in some way controls all forms of mass media directly. Therefore, the authority for all mass communications is in the hands of a small group of party leaders. This theory is derived from the ideologies of Marx and Engel that "the ideas of the ruling classes are the ruling ideas". It was thought that the entire mass media was saturated with bourgeois ideology. Lenin thought of private ownership as being incompatible with freedom of press and that modern technological means of information must be controlled for enjoying effective freedom of press. The theory advocated that the sole purpose of mass media was to educate the great masses of workers and not to give out information. The public was encouraged to give feedback as it was the only way the media would be able to cater to its interests.

The media according to this theory play down everything bad under communism while play up everything bad in democratic countries. For example, the Soviet media did not emphasize accidents like train wrecks and boat sinking or natural disasters. Why? Because it made the government look bad. At the same time the media in the Soviet Union played up the bad news in democratic countries—especially the United States. This made democracies look like as if they were not working. A great example of this theory is the disdain communists tend to have for democracy. Here's a good example from Fidel Castro. In a speech in 1991, Castro referred to democracy as "complete garbage."

The great change came after Mikhail Gorbachev came to power in 1985 and started on a plan that was to eventually cause the Soviet Union to be no more. Two concepts introduced by Gorbachev: *Perestroika*: restructuring of society and the economy and *Glasnost*: openness. While Gorbachev was still in power, he changed the way the state broadcast monopoly worked and gave greater authority to local governments and professionals.

It must be added that Russia and most of the former Soviet republics have had a difficult time making it in the transition from communism to democracy. And some of the reforms have not lasted. In Russia, crime is rampant. A strong mob element that had existed under communism that simply took over areas of the economy. And the government has exercised more and more control over the media. The countries that follow the communist line are dwindling. Still, many are left. Each exists in its own unique situation. North Korea, China, Cuba and Vietnam are the best examples of the Soviet/Communist system in existence today. By far the best example is North Korea under the dictator Kim Jong Il. Each of the other countries—China, Cuba and Vietnam provides insights into the communist system at work.

2.2.3 The Libertarian Theory

This is also known as the 'Free Press Theory'. During the Age of Reason in 17th century, another theory, libertarianism, evolved in United States initiated by the forerunners John Milton, Thomas Jefferson and John Stuart Mill. Libertarianism grants a totally free press upholding that people are inherently rational truth-seekers. Journalists and broadcasters have this freedom of expression as stated in the First Amendment ("Congress shall pass no law...abridging the freedom of speech, or of the press."). Though sometimes it leads to some libel and slander cases in the part of journalists, yet they have this freedom to defend themselves. We have what we call the privileged communication and fair comment on matters of public interest.

This movement is based on the right of an individual, and advocates absence of restraint. The basis of this theory dates back to 17th century England when the printing press made it possible to print several copies of a book or pamphlet at cheap rates. The State was thought of as a major source of interference on the rights of an individual and his property. Libertarians regarded taxation as institutional theft. Popular will (*vox populi*) was granted precedence over the power of State.

Advocates of this theory were Lao Tzu, an early 16th century philosopher, John Locke of Great Britain in the 17th century, John Milton, the epic poet (*Aeropagitica*) and John Stuart Mill, an essayist (*On Liberty*). Milton in *Aeropagitica* in 1644, referred to a self-righting process if free expression is permitted "let truth and falsehood grapple." In 1789, the French, in their *Declaration of the Rights of Man*, wrote "Every citizen may speak, write and publish freely." Out of such doctrines came the idea of a "free marketplace of ideas." George Orwell defined libertarianism as "allowing people to say things you do not want to hear". Libertarians argued that the press should be seen as the *Fourth Estate* reflecting public opinion. In short, what the theory offers, in sum, is power without social responsibility.

The best early expression of libertarian ideals is *Areopagitica*, an essay published by John Milton in 1644. In the essay, which was intended for Parliament, Milton argued for intellectual freedom without government control.[5] In America, the best example historically of libertarian thought was Thomas Jefferson.[6] The best spokesman for Libertarian thought was John Stuart Mill.[7]

To put this into perspective: we've never had a complete libertarian system existing for any length of time in any country except in times of war or civil unrest. We do have a Libertarian Party here in the United States. This is not the same as the Libertarian Theory of the Press, although similarities do exist. To a certain extent, a form of social libertarianism is practiced in The Netherlands, and in some of the Scandinavian countries. It exists to a lesser extent in places such as Hungary.

2.2.4 Social Responsibility Theory

Critics of the Free Press Theory were Wilbur Schramm, Siebert and Theodore Paterson. In their book *Four Theories of Press*, they stated "pure libertarianism is antiquated, outdated and obsolete." They advocated the need for its replacement by the Social Responsibility theory. This theory can be said to have been initiated in the United States by the Commission of The Freedom of Press, 1949. The commission found that the free market approach to press freedom had only increased the power of a single class and has not served the interests of the less well-off classes. The emergence of radio, TV and film suggested the need for some means of accountability. Thus, the theory advocated some obligation on the part of the media to society. A judicial mix of self-regulation and state regulation and high professional standards were imperative. Social Responsibility theory thus became the modern variation in which the duty to one's conscience was the primary basis of the right of free expression.

Social Responsibility provides for private ownership of mass media in exchange for responsible use of that media. Social Responsibility is tied to a form of government that is based on the Constitution and the Bill of Rights. In theory, we have a free marketplace of ideas that coincides with capitalism and the free-enterprise system. We couldn't have free-enterprise without that. And, we couldn't have a free press without the free enterprise system to back it up. This is so because controls in one area would mean controls in other areas too. Media according to this theory is supposed to be of the highest standard of social responsibility. This theory is applicable in countries such as the United States, Canada, Great Britain, France, Germany, Italy, Israel, Australia, New Zealand, Japan, the Philippines, India, etc. Many nations in Latin America and elsewhere practice democracy, but the concept of press freedom is a fragile one.

2.3 AUTHORITARIAN POLITICAL ARCHITECTURE IN MYANMAR

Out of the four theories mentioned above, the authoritarian theory best suits the mass media model in Myanmar. According to Siebert (1963), "it is a theory under which the press, as an institution, is controlled in its functions and operation by organized society through another institution, i.e. the government" (p. 10). For almost five decades after the imposition of military rule in 1962, the press has been dominated by the military regime in Myanmar. The regime has adopted the basic principles of authoritarianism for controlling almost all aspect of the mass media. This has been reflected in institutions and authority structures that have developed in Myanmar in the last half a century.

Myanmar's politics in the post-colonial era has undergone tremendous changes. Beginning with parliamentary model in 1948 and after the army seized power in Myanmar in 1962, there has been series of extended power struggles within the different groups in the society. During this prolonged rule of successive military regimes under different nomenclatures, military junta seems to have endured under its often contested institutions and history. The importance of authoritarian institutions such as party, military, and state apparatuses, in sustaining non-democratic rule is significant. Under this background, this section looks into these structures of authoritarianism in Myanmar.

2.3.1 State Apparatus

A primary goal of the founders of independent Myanmar was to create a government blending the values and ideas of liberal democracy inherited from the British with the socialist values and goals expressed in evolutionary socialism. The liberal tradition provided the basic idea underlying the Constitution that power emanated from the people. The socialist basis was reflected by the imposition of certain limitations such as expropriation of the private property in accordance with law (Silverstein 1977: 54-55). The structure of the government followed the British Parliamentary model. For eighteen months, Myanmar experimented with constitutional authoritarian government under the leadership of General Ne Win.

Military rule was established in Myanmar by the coup in March 1962. Following the coup, all powers were assumed by the Revolutionary Council, which in turn conferred all legislative, executive and judicial power on its Chairman Ne Win. The line between the Revolutionary Council and the government was undefined and the members of the Revolutionary Council were also the ministers in the government. This pattern persisted through most of this phase of military rule (Steinberg 1981; 1982). In 1971, the formal government assumed a more traditional façade. After the first Congress of the BSPP it was announced that a new Constitution would be written which finally completed its task in 1973. Subsequently, a constitutional dictatorship was established under the control of Burma Socialist Programme Party (BSPP) (Taylor 2005: 23). The Constitution sought to continue the goals it undertook following the coup in 1962, i.e. direct control over the entire nation through a strong and disciplined administrative structure (Silverstein 1977: 133).

Since the collapse of Ne Win's personalistic authoritarian military regime in 1988, several attempts have been made to accommodate Myanmar's diverse political forces on the nature of political transition from military to civilian rule, but so far no significant results have been achieved (Pederson 2005: 162). The military government effectively annulled the 1990 election following a landslide victory for NLD, and work on a new Constitution which began in 1993 was abandoned three years later when NLD withdrew from the military controlled National Convention (Taylor 2005: 23). The government has since then announced a seven point 'roadmap' and holding of fresh multi-party elections in 2010. The experience of the two decades in Myanmar shows that the people within the government and the NLD, as well as most ethnic nationalist organizations recognizes that the only viable way forward is a gradual transition, which accommodates vital interests on all sides.

The BSPP's monopoly in controlling the state meant that the singular route to the control of state resources lay with the party. Politics, according to Than (2007: 162), resembled a 'triangle of accommodation' in which the party assumed the pre-eminent position. It relied on military for support in realising its goals through the state apparatus. Personnel were co-opted into the party hierarchy through their selection from state and military establishments. The unabated insurgency also enhanced military's role. Attempts were made to undermine the ethnic conflicts that continued to threaten the unity of the union (Taylor 2005: 18).

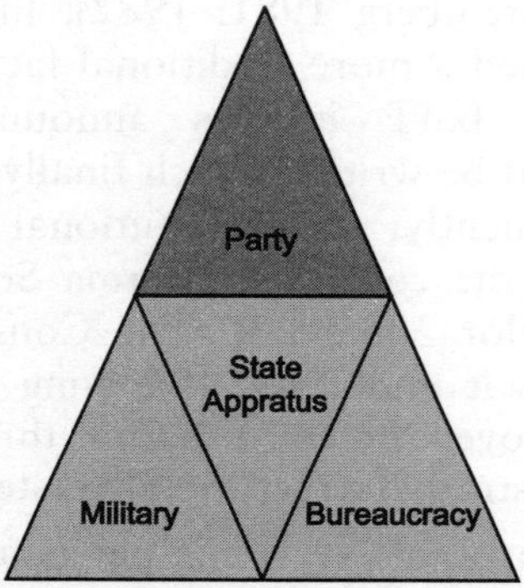

Fig. 2.2: Triangular Axis of State Apparatus.

Source: Than, Tin Maung Maung (2007), *State Dominance in Myanmar: The Political Economy of Industrialisation*, ISEAS, p. 162.

In an attempt to civilianize the government about twenty key military officers were forced to resign and assume civilian titles. However, this effort to govern has been alleged as a camouflage for continued military control (Steinberg 1981: 70). Although military was devoid of its formal political role, its influence in the governance of the country remained undiminished (Than 2007: 162). In fact, the party and the political leadership comprised of the paramount position of Ne Win as Chairman of the BSPP, the Chairman of the Council of State, and finally as the head of the military (Hlaing 2008: 157). Although formally subscribing to the BSPP's political role, the party organisation within the armed forces was structured to ensure that the chain of command was not compromised—beginning from ward and village level to township and state level. The military formed an important component of people's council at each level and also is a major element of Pyithu Hluttaw—Peoples Assembly, as well as of the BSPP itself (Steinberg 1981: 70).

In order to establish one-party authoritarianism Ne Win sought to use the BSPP to cement the allegiance of civil servants and others to his military backed regime. The party membership was open to all. Party members took over many of the administrative posts at all levels of government, and civil servants were expected to become its members (Fink 2001: 37). Increasing bureaucratisation resulted in a privileged class, even as more professionals and technocrats were co-opted into the system. Although this trinity of state-party-military appeared to have instituted political stability and ensured regime security by consolidating its political structure, in reality, the BSPP could not forestall the building up of systemic weaknesses associated with one-party dominance in an authoritarian setting (Than 2007: 163).

2.3.2 Economy

The economic objective of the *Burmese Way to Socialism* was to establish a socialistic economy that entailed "participation of all for the general well-being in works of common ownership.... Socialist economy, according to the document, aimed at the establishment of a new society for all, economically secure and morally better, to live in peace and prosperity" (Burmese Way to Socialism, 1962). Self-reliance and economic independence were stressed as essential elements of socialist economic strategy. The main thrust of the Revolutionary Council's was oriented towards establishing state control over the 'commanding heights' of the national economy through nationalization and regulation of the private sector, while attempting to considerably expand state-owned enterprises (Than 2007: 114). On the whole rapid expansion of the socialist structure was envisaged.

After the military coup of 1962, General Ne Win's promotion of *The Burmese Way to Socialism* embarked the country upon a catastrophic programme of international isolation and autarchy (McCarthy 2000a: 234). The economy was characterized by near isolation from the international system and stagnant growth. Foreign firms were the first to feel the effects of the new policy of Burmanisation of the economy. All foreign and private banks were nationalized. Ne Win further stipulated that the state would nationalize the production, distribution, import and export of all major commodities. The overall economic direction meant state ownership of the basic means of production (Steinberg 1982: 77). The wave of nationalization was so intense and severe that according to Bala, "it resulted in an army dominated state. Even the pan shops were nationalized".[8] Between 1963-65, all banks, industries and large shops were nationalized (Fink 2001: 32). This policy of economic nationalism, according to Sundhaussen (1995: 775) resulted in 'economic xenophobia'. In May 1964, currency was demonetized (50 kyat and 100 kyat) forcing large amount of cash out of private control. Most of the businesses were run by Indian and Chinese. The regulation of the currency, trade and production restrictions forced hundreds and thousands of Indian and Chinese people leaving the country (Steinberg 1981: 35; 1982: 77-79). Furthermore, the private sector was emasculated both by regulations on private ownership and exclusion of private sector from institutionalized credit and other resources (Than 2007: 144).

In April 1964, the government established a Socialist Economic Construction Committee (SECC). Nationalisation of trade and industry was one of the steps in the construction of a Socialist State. The rapid action of socializing and nationalizing the commercial and industrial sector of the economy produced shortages, rising prices and black markets (Silverstein 1977: 156). By 1966, the economic situation had not improved and dissatisfaction increased. In spite of the articulated goals of centralized planning and nationalization of means of production and trade, the policy of economic nationalism failed miserably under Revolutionary Council (Steinberg 1981: 36). Corruption expanded with state control, production fell and imports of these commodities dropped. Black market came to be known as 'Corporation 24', as there were 23 other state corporations (quoted in Steinberg 1981: 37). Private capital had very few legal avenues of economic investment. Smuggling came to play an important role in the economy and the easiest way to make money.

The economy was largely influenced by the decline state of agriculture. While land reform programmes carried through by the regime gave agricultural plots to many landless farmers, but the farmers were told from now onwards to sell their produce to the government at below market prices. This frustrated the farmers and they started putting less effort in cultivation which resulted in dramatic reduction in the rice exports from the country (Fink 2001). By 1967, there was a serious crisis in the agricultural sector. Exports fell as a result of poor government procurement, and scarcities arose both in foodstuff and household necessities including clothing (Steinberg 1981: 36). At the national level, the denial of the market forces and the marginalization of the private sector impaired the country's robustness for sustained growth. The slow progress of the manufacturing sector, which had absorbed one-third of state investments and yet whose labour productivity was below the national average, aggravated the problems of economic stagnation in the second half of the 1980s (Than 2007: 275). The socio-economic situation continues to deteriorate in Myanmar.

The current military regime has tried to reverse the deteriorating socio-economic conditions and introduced several market-oriented reforms. The Union of Myanmar Foreign Investment Law was promulgated on 30 November 1988, as The State Law and Order Restoration Council Law No. 10/88, in order to promote all-round development of national economy. This has allowed private sector businesses to engage in external trade and to retain export earnings, and started to legitimize and formalize border trade with neighboring countries, hitherto an activity that had been deemed illegal. Following this, "Myanmar's economy was released from the isolationist foreign policy of the quarter-century long Socialist era and began to re-integrate into regional and world markets" (Kudo and Mieno 2007). However, the benefits have accrued primarily to a small privileged elite and have not translated into broad-based improvements in the standard of living (Pederson 2005: 163). According to the Myanmar analysts, growing direct foreign investment, strong economic growth, and economic reforms, in Myanmar, has led to inflation. It has outstripped the rate of GDP growth by three to four times, indicating the lack of genuine reforms introduced by the military rulers.

Through this open trade policy, volume of external trade has increased substantially in Myanmar. Imports, however, grew more rapidly than the exports resulting in the trade deficits. In spite of the foreign economic sanctions, Foreign Direct Investment (FDI) in Myanmar has significantly contributed to the development and growth of a liberalized neo-patrimonial economic regime. When taking a closer look at the European sanctions towards Myanmar, it becomes obvious that they have never had an economic impact. The European Union (EU) implemented an investment ban on Myanmar but made exceptions for the oil and gas industries, which constitute Myanmar's most important sector for international investment. French and German oil companies have a major stake in Burmese energy resources. Despite the European arms embargo, their assistance extends to providing technical assistance and advice with regard to military activities.

The country now after the 2010 elections is on a drive to attract investment, promoting tourism, timber, gemstones and its vast oil and gas reserves. In this regard, a "Special Economic Zone Law" was passed on January 27, 2011 to attract much-needed foreign capital to an economy held back by decades of sanctions and mismanagement. The new investment law follows a series of reforms undertaken over the past year, including the privatisation of hundreds of state assets, and plans to expand banking, telecommunications, shipping and agricultural sectors. Even Nobel laureate Suu Kyi has appealed for the support of the Burmese cause and establishment of a just political and economic order in Myanmar (Kyi, 2011).

2.3.3 Party Machinery

Although the Revolutionary Council had a monopoly of power, it needed to win and hold public support. The Council realized this from the beginning that it had to establish contact with the people and win their loyalty if it was to convert its authoritarian rule into a more democratic form (Silverstein 1977: 100). Faced with this dilemma, the Council announced in July 1962 that it was creating a new party to be known as Burma Socialist Programme Party (BSPP—*Lanzin* Party in Burmese). In making the announcement, the Council expressed the hope that members of the old parties would be able to discard their partisan feelings and come closer for unity and understanding through intimate exchange of views. As the regime began to solidify its control, the civilian parties were pushed into the background. By March 1964, all political parties except the BSPP were finally banned (Steinberg 1981: 31).

The BSPP was to be a transitional party under the leadership of the Revolutionary Council and its purpose was to lead the country towards the ideological goals expressed in the *Burmese Way to Socialism*. At its early stage of development, it was to be a cadre party with emphasis upon identifying, indoctrinating members who assist the military rulers in carrying out their programmes (Silverstein 1977: 101). It remained a cadre party until 1971, when it was transformed into mass national party and given the responsibility of drawing up the new constitution and the opportunity to assume the leadership of the nation.

After the dissolution of BSPP, it was replaced by National Unity Party (NUP) which was formed on September 26, 1988, through the intervention of the SLORC. The NUP was intended to serve as an electoral vehicle for SLORC in the polls held in 1990. In the polls that followed, NUP captured only ten seats in the Peoples' Assembly of the 485 seats. Subsequently, in the National Convention that was instituted, NUP participated as the unpopular instrument of the resented military (Leifer 2001: 199). According to Smith (1999: 20), it was in fact, "the former BSPP disguised in new clothes without any serving military members". Allied to the NUP were a number of smaller satellite parties made up of former BSPP supporters. It also inherited the buildings, property and registration lists of the BSPP (Smith 1999: 21). The party had a distinct financial advantage because it was able to take over many of the BSPP offices and equipments for free (Fink 2001: 63). It soon became clear that the regime hoped to engineer the elections of 1990 so that the NUP could have an outright victory.

The Union Solidarity and Development Association (USDA) was formed by the military to woo the masses on September 15, 1993. Although purportedly a social organization, USDA was officially headed by General Than Swe and was often used to defend the interests of the regime (Fink 2001: 95). Since its formation in 1993, however, and particularly in recent years the SPDC has been pursuing an internal strategy intended to make it the post-SPDC civilian political vehicle (Smith 1999: 429). The USDA is also taking a greater informal role in local administration. The military is instructed to work in close cooperation with the USDA on irrigation, agriculture, economic issues and transportation in the regions, and central instructions have been for them to be present at all opening ceremonies of dams and bridges and so on, wearing USDA uniforms (Bowman 2007: 8). Although established in 1993, membership of USDA has quickly risen to several million people. According to Bala, "Less educated people were, particularly, drawn towards USDA, believing it was really working for the country".[9] However, in several districts peoples' names were simply added to the membership list without ever being consulted. And it was virtually impossible to become a civil servant without first joining the USDA.

The state supported political party with strong military ties —the Union Solidarity and Development Party (USDP) grew out of the USDA, which was a regime-created organization that has received substantial government support since its formation in 1993 (NDI 2010: 5). The USDA was transformed into USDP on 29 March 2010. In the post-election politics, USDP has dominated the National Parliament and the state/region assemblies.

The National Democratic Force (NDF) was formed as a breakaway group from Suu Kyi's NLD party, which was forced to disband following its decision not to run in the 2010 elections. According to NDF supporters, "the boycott of elections by Aung San Suu Kyi's party is meaningless and will only aid the military government".

2.3.4 Armed Forces

As the army grew and consolidated its political and economic power during the 1950s in the wake of civil war and divisions among nationalist forces, it became more than a pillar of the post-colonial state. As Taylor (2005: 15) argues, it became 'state's guarantor and protector' or as Callahan (2001: 429) argues—transformation took place in the role of the 'military as institution' into 'military as government'. It also developed its own ideology for the future direction of the state. This was profoundly influenced by the three interacting forces of—Nationalism, Socialism and Buddhism—which was enshrined in the three critical documents, *The Burmese Way to Socialism*; *The System of Correlation of Man and his Environment*; and the *Constitution of the BSPP* (Steinberg 1982: 35). Each of them complimented the other creating a pattern of socialist policy that continues to be paramount.

Military junta which replaced parliamentary regime through a coup organized by Revolutionary Council on March 2, 1962, abolished the 1962 Constitution and ruled through decree. The populace was completely depoliticized and socialist revolution became the vanguard of state ideology. The Revolutionary Council's rule was characterised by unprecedented power and autonomy for the state which became synonymous with the ruling military junta. Ruling by decree, the Revolutionary Council was able to impose its authority over the polity (Than 2007: 111, 113).

Ever since the creation of the State Law and Order Restoration Council (SLORC) in September 1988, the Burmese armed forces have been engaged in an ambitious expansion and modernisation program. Despite the country's chronic economic and social problems, reduced internal security concerns and lack of external threats, this program is continuing under the SLORC's successor, the State Peace and Development Council (SPDC), which was created in November 1997 (Sleth 2001: 1).

Over the past 20 years, the regime has made a major effort to expand and modernise Myanmar's military, consistently reserving about 35 per cent of the national budget to this end. After decades of being a small, lightly armed infantry force geared to regime protection and counter-insurgency, Myanmar now boasts a large, reasonably well-integrated, well-armed, tri-service defence force capable of limited conventional military operations. These increased capabilities raise the stakes faced by a hostile neighbour and help act as a deterrent against invasion (Sleth 2008: 281-97).

The militarized State has near total control of all other non-military institutions from the economic and cultural sector to civil society, industry and media. Even the educational system—both higher and a secondary level and the market forces—the Chamber of Commerce and think tanks are all working under the close supervision of the military. The state engulfed by military is still in its pre-modern stage dominated by feudal and patrimonial tendencies. Recognised by class formations which are primarily feudal, the military has cut across all the levels of the society. After the end of the BSPP regime, the country has moved towards 'marketisation' which is in stark contrast to the 'Burmanisation' programme of the Ne Win era. This economic reform carried out by the military junta has given rise to 'crony capitalism'. According to Maung Maung Zarni, "the pie is to divided amongst the cronies who, inter alia, serve as the generals portfolio managers" (Zarni 2010). Institutionally, since the early 1990s, "the military has its hand in virtually every economic pie, from poultry farms, small factories, real estate, tourism, transportation, construction, rental business of regimental facilities to shipping, power, banking, export and import, agriculture, energy and mining" (*ibid.*). No business entity of commercial significance can operate without being linked to the military, institutionally or to individual commanders, thereby bringing the market forces of the society under the *Tatmadaw's* effective control.

The power from the junta was handed over to the civilian government after the November 2010 elections. The election was, however, a highly controlled and managed affair. The presence of the military alongside the 80 per cent of elected seats won by the USDP, which is backed by the ruling junta, means that prospects of a true civilian government are unlikely.

2.3.5 Elections

Authoritarian rulers may deploy a wide range of strategies to keep control over their agents, as well as their adversaries, in various institutional arenas. In electoral authoritarian regimes, election constitutes the central arena of struggle (Schedler 2010: 71). They have at their disposal a broad array of manipulative tools for reducing the uncertainty that elections can bring such as disempowerment, market restrictions, preference alteration and vote distortions (*ibid.*: 73). The 2010 elections in Myanmar, were the fifth step "Roadmap to Democracy" as announced by the military junta in 2002. The electoral administration was appointed unilaterally by the regime on March 11, 2010, and soon showed itself to heavily favor the regime and its allies. The Union Election Commission (UEC) lacked independence; the SPDC directly appointed its members with no public input. Political parties had to register with the Union Election Commission and request permission to run. The election laws were developed by the military government and effectively prohibited longstanding opponents of the regime from contesting the elections. One of the laws, on political party registration, resulted in the silencing of many of the most prominent opposition voices.

The election law required all political parties to reregister in order to remain in existence and compete in the elections. But parties could do so only if none of their members were currently imprisoned based on a court conviction. This requirement presented parties with a choice of either expelling prominent imprisoned members, or declining to reregister. Many countries demanded the release of Myanmar's democratic icon, and Nobel Laureate, Daw Aung San Suu Kyi, and her full participation in the election. However, the National League for Democracy soon announced it would boycott the election rather than expel its leader.

Eventually, 47 political parties attempted to register. The UEC initially approved 42 to contest the elections. However, the commission then dissolved five of the parties, leaving 37 approved parties and over 80 individual candidates. By Election Day, 23 parties remained to participate in the elections. Many ethnic politicians saw this election as a rare opportunity to campaign for ethnic rights and democracy. Therefore, they formed new parties to run in the elections. Some ethnic armed groups agreed to be transformed into members of the junta-controlled Border Guard Force (BGF).

The Censorship Board (The Press Scrutiny and Registration Board, or PSRB) issued a directive prohibiting all weekly publications in the country from publishing any commentary or analysis on the electoral laws. Also, the approved political parties needed to apply for permission from the PSRB within 90 days after registering with the UEC for permission to print their own campaign materials. Each party had also to deposit 500,000 kyats (USD 500) with the PSRB.

The UEC announced nine restrictions for campaign speeches, while also limiting each party to 15 minutes of media airtime each. Media organizations and political parties faced numerous obstacles such as only having 15 minutes of airtime for the entire campaign, restrictions, communications and Internet slowdowns, threats of punishment, and cyber attacks. The SPDC's Union Election Commission held the elections on November 7, 2010. During the election period, it became increasingly clear that the use of advance votes obtained through coerced voting or outright fraud was a major problem. These advance votes were often taken before the official advance voting period of November 5-6. This advance voting seems to be part of a systematic operation to give the USDP an insurmountable lead before Election Day. These ballots were generally collected in every manner possible, often relying on proxy voting, ghost voting, or coerced voting using threats and intimidation. Allegations of fraud and counting/advance voting irregularities were common. The voter turnout was 76.48 per cent, in which a vast majority of the seats in Parliament were won by the USDP.

On 16 September 2010, the UEC issued notification No. 99, No. 100, No. 101, No. 102, and No. 103. In these notifications, the Union Election Commission announced that, according to Article 8(f) of the Union Election Commission Law, voting will not be held in some areas in Kachin, Shan, Karenni, Karen and Mon states because they are in no position to host free and fair elections in the Multiparty Democracy General Elections to be held on 7 November 2010. This will affect about 300 village-tracts in 32 townships in 5 States. Therefore, hundreds of thousands of people cannot vote in this election. So, the ethnic political parties will lose votes in these areas.

Except the USDP and NUP, most political parties have complained about the short campaign period and a lack of funds. According to the regime's party registration laws, parties must submit a list of party members to the UEC within 90 days of being approved as political party. If a party intends to contest nationwide, it must submit a list of 1000 party members, but if the party is going to contest only in a State or region, it must submit a list of 500 party members. Some political parties have faced problems when they campaign. For example, the SNDP party was prevented by local authorities from campaigning in Loikaw. Burmese junta crony businessman, Htay Myint, a USDP candidate in Myeik Township, Tanintharyi Region, has reached a price-cutting deal with local electricity suppliers for his constituents, as part of his electoral campaign. It is a ploy to buy support from local voters.

The USDP has organized the Rohingya community in Maungdaw, Arakan State, to gain their support by issuing a National Identity Card (White card). It is the only way for Rohingya residents to obtain the card. As well, the USDP has been discretely collecting new member signatures from residents of Mudon and Thanphyuzayart townships, Mon State, during September. Adding their signatures to the party's membership list serves as a commitment the signers will vote for the party in the upcoming elections. Some government officials have been canvassing for votes along with candidates of the USDP in their respective area. But, according to the election laws, government staff shall not get involved in political campaigning. More interestingly, the regime has collected over 70,000 names of voters in four areas near the China-Myanmar border, in northeast Shan State, and ordered them to vote for the government backed USDP. The USDP party has recruited Burmese business tycoons as party candidates. Therefore, the USDP party has enough funds and human resources to pay for their campaign. On the other hand, some opposition parties attempted to raise funds by collecting donations at markets, but the local municipal committee tried to stop these activities.

2.3.6 The Closed Media

Myanmar is one of the countries in the world that has no media freedom under dictatorship. There are many laws restricting the press in Myanmar. Censorship is a fact of life in Myanmar. The Censorship Board is very important and pervasive. All private journals are required to submit every one of their articles for approval before publication. If journalists do not follow the laws, their journalist licenses are taken away.

The absence of media freedom is one of the major challenges for democratization process in Myanmar. In Myanmar, military regime has used the propaganda and censorship as a very effective weapon in governing the country. Military junta uses propaganda as an effective weapon for stability of their power and to persuade ignorant public to be their force (Myay 2011). In 1962, General Ne Win seized the State power and started establishment of censor ship body. It was called as press scrutiny board which had to strict on print media especially at that time. It also had intention to overwhelm the political rights and civil liberties too. It was the very early oppression of media freedom. No print media as well as television broadcasting could come out without strict censorship. Even, the video cassette tapes and movies need censorship. In general, the whole media had been monopolized, overwhelmed by military junta since then.

On the other hand, the military rulers also used their propaganda on all State-owned media as the most effective tool to create a socio-political environment where the citizens were ignorant of politics, blinded their knowledge of citizen rights and democratization process. People in the rural areas are the most vulnerable due to their tendency to easily fall into regime's propaganda trap and psychological warfare. As a consequence the tendency of social and ideological divide among Burmese community continued in Myanmar.

After the military junta announced its plans to hold elections in Myanmar, the PSRB issued a directive on March 8, 2010, prohibiting all weekly publications in the country from publishing any comments or analysis on the electoral laws being announced daily through the state-owned media. The Censorship Board took another step on July 20 when it issued a directive prohibiting journals from publishing discussion or analysis of the 2008 constitution or the 2010 election laws with the threat that failure to comply would result in the journals losing their publishing license.

On March 17, 2010, the military junta announced that political parties would have to register for permission to print any election-related materials with the government following the 1962 Printers and Publishers Registration Act. According to this act, each political party would need to seek permission from the Censorship Board within 90 days after registering with the Election Commission. If the political parties would like to publish, the parties would have to deposit 500,000 kyats (US$ 500) for permission to print. The government's UEC issued a notice on September 14 granting "legal"parties the right to campaign on state-run radio and television, with 15 minutes allotted for each campaign speech by their chairmen or secretaries before October 25, 2010. The draft copy of their speeches, as expected, had to be approved in advance by the Censorship Board.

Though the opposition parties were denied access to the state's broadcasting facilities, candidates were still able to spread their campaign messages through private publications.[10] Myanmar embassies in foreign countries did not issue visas for foreign journalists. U Thein Soe, the commission chairman, said the country did not need any foreign journalists or outside observers. On the other hand, 25 Burmese journalists, who worked for the foreign media, along with two Chinese correspondents, were allowed to cover the polls. Local reporters working for foreign media said that Burmese police and security agents followed them, monitored their movements, and photographed them when they went about covering the election management.

A reporter, Hla Hla Win, was sentenced on December 31, 2009 to 20 years' imprisonment for violating the Electronics Act, and an additional seven years for violation of the Import-Export Act, 5(1). She is now serving her term at Myitkyina prison in Kachin State. Another (undercover) reporter from the Democratic Voice of Burma (DVB) was sentenced to a total of 13 years in 2010. Reporter Ngwe Soe Lin was given a 10-year jail sentence for violating Section 33(a) of the Electronics Act, and an additional three years for violating Section 13(1) of the Immigration Emergency Provisions Act. A journalist, Maung Zeya, and his son were arrested by the police on April 17, 2010, after Maung Zeya's son took pictures of the sites of three bomb explosions in Rangoon. The blasts, which happened two days earlier, resulted in 10 people killed and 170 wounded. Aung Thu Nyein, 28, an intern for *Weekly Eleven Journal*, was arrested on September 13, 2010, for taking photos of the flooding that hit Magwe in central Myanmar.

Apart from arrests and intimidation of journalists, the military junta intentionally launched 'cyber attacks' in the lead up to the elections against the websites of Burmese exiled media, including The Irrawaddy, Mizzima, and DVB. These media organizations suffered from DDoS (Distributed Denial of Service) attacks that temporarily shut down their websites. A week before the election, Internet speed in Rangoon was severely slowed down. Internet cafés had to close due to the abnormally slow connections that frustrated many customers. Connection speeds in other parts of Myanmar, including Arakan, Kachin, and Karen States, and Tenasserim, Mandalay and Sagaing Divisions, were also reported to be very slow. The military junta always attempts to control the media by imposing laws and regulations. However, inside and exiled media made attempts to cover the election news as much as possible. Apart from media, CBOs and NGOs monitored the elections and documented information related to the election. These CBOs and NGOs included ANFREL (Asia Network for Free and Fair Elections), HRDP (Human Rights Defenders and Promoters), BNI (Burma News International), BP (Burma Partnership), ND-Burma (Network for Human Rights Documentation, Burma), BNHR (Burma Network for Human Rights), and HURFOM (Human Rights Foundation of Monland). These organizations issued statements, published reports, news, and interviews about the elections, as well as human rights abuses committed during the election period.

Those laws, in place since a military coup in 1962, include edicts prohibiting journalists from writing articles that could threaten peace and stability, oppose the constitution or insult ethnic groups. Critics say some laws are open to interpretation and give the government enormous power to silence dissent. They have been used repeatedly in recent years to jail members of the press. Myanmar's reporters had long been regarded as among the most restricted in the world. But President Thein Sein's reformist government has significantly relaxed media controls since 2011, allowing reporters to print material that would have been unthinkable during the era of absolute military rule—such as photographs of Aung San Suu Kyi when she was under house arrest in Rangoon.

However, the remnants of old regime was still seen when, in June 2012, the government's Press Scrutiny and Registration Department ordered the suspension of a magazine called *Snapshot*. It was reported that *Snapshot* had published a photo of a woman who was raped and murdered in Arakan State, igniting a wave of violence in the remote region of western Myanmar. In July, the censor board again showed its strength by ordering the suspension of two weekly magazines, the *Voice Weekly* and *Envoy*, for speculating on a still-anticipated cabinet reshuffle. Those punishments have since been lifted, and the two magazines are due to begin publishing again on 18 August 2012.

On August 20, a Ministry of Information official announced that editors of news publications would no longer have to submit stories to the censorship board ahead of publication. This unprecedented reform eliminates a draconian provision that has been in place since the PSRD was established in 1964 by Myanmar's then military regime. The new rules will impact a range of news and religious journals that have been heavily censored up to this point. However, editors will still be held accountable for the content and required to adhere to sixteen guidelines. Some of these are loosely worded and prohibit reporting on issues deemed "sensitive" and would ban stories that "harm national security" or the "dignity of the state."

Recently, a provisional Myanmar Press Council (MPC) has been formed to consider media affairs before a new media law is formally enacted by the Burmese Parliament. The reformation of the provisional press council comes after protests from domestic journalists who called for more say in the national press council. The provisional council consists of twenty-nine members and includes retired Supreme Court Judge Khin Maung Aye as chairman, Soe Thein, a noted writer and journalist, as vice-chairman, and chief editor of the private *Voice Weekly* journal Kyaw Min Swe as secretary. The press council also includes members of the Myanmar Writers Association, Myanmar Journalist Association, Myanmar Printing and Publishing Entrepreneurs Association, Myanmar Publishers Association, Myanmar Press Union, Myanmar Journalists Network and others.

Notes

1. The literature on totalitarianism is extensive. The classical definition and explanation are found in Hannah Arendt (1966), *The Origins of Totalitarianism*, New York: Harcourt Brace; Fredrich, Carl J. and Z. Brzezinski (1956), Totalitarianism, *Dictatorship and Democracy*, New York: Fredrick A. Praeger; Jacob L. Talmon, *The Rise of Totalitarian Democracy*, Boston: The Beacon Press, 1952.
2. Soe Myint is the editor of *Mizimma News*. This is based on the interview with Soe Myint.

3. The cultural elements of the pre-colonial Myanmar kept the junta's determination to keep things unchanged. They draw on very old anxieties, deeply rooted in their cultural history (Mathews 1999: 79).

4. This was evident in the imposition of modern system of communication, law and order and rational government.

5. He said:

   "...though all the winds of doctrine were let loose to play upon the earth, so truth be in the field.... Let her (truth) and falsehood grapple; who ever knew truth put to the worse, in a free and open encounter?"

6. In a letter, he wrote in 1787, Jefferson said:

   "The basis of our government being the opinion of the people, the very first object should be to keep that right; and were it left to me to decide whether we should have a government without newspapers or newspapers without a government, I should not hesitate a moment to prefer the latter."

   Jefferson also said:

   "Eternal vigilance is the price of liberty."

   That quote is on the right side at the entrance to the National Archives Building in Washington.

7. In 1859, he wrote in *On Liberty*:

   "When we consider either the history of opinion or the ordinary conduct of human life, to what is it to be ascribed that the one and the other are no worse than they are? Not certainly to the inherent force of the human understanding, for on any matter not self-evident there are ninety-nine persons totally incapable of judging of it for one who is capable; and the capacity of the hundredth person is only comparative, for the majority of the eminent men of every past generation held many opinions now known to be erroneous, and did or approved numerous things which no one will now justify. Why is it, then, that there is on the whole a preponderance among mankind of rational opinions and rational conduct? If there really is this preponderance—which there must be unless human affairs are, and have always been, in an almost desperate state—it is owing to a quality of the human mind, the source of everything respectable in man either as an intellectual or as a moral being, namely, that his errors are corrigible."

8. Based on interview with Bala, '1988 Generation' Student Activist.

9. Based on Interview.

10. Restrictions were imposed on campaign speeches which were broadcast on state-run media. Some of these restrictions included the following:

    1. Must not include any speech that can lead to disintegration of the Union or national solidarity, or be detrimental to national sovereignty.

2. Must not include any speech that can harm security, the rule of law, or community peace.
3. Must not disobey the Constitution (2008) of the Union of Myanmar (Burma) or any existing laws.
4. Must not stimulate sedition or include any speech that can tarnish the image of the state.
5. Must not include any speech that can lead to the collapse of the Tatmadaw (armed forces) or tarnish the image of the Tatmadaw.
6. Must not include any speech or undertake organizing measures that can lead to conflicts or harm the dignity or moral conduct in connection with racism or religion or affairs of an individual or community.
7. Must not abuse religion for political ends.
8. Must not include any speech that can harm the peaceful pursuit of education.
9. Must not include any speech that can discourage service personnel from performing their duties or to abet them to stage protests against the government.

Chapter 3

Military Rule in Myanmar

3.1 POST-COLONIAL DEVELOPMENTS

The key to a contemporary understanding of the prospects for democratisation lies in the understanding of the role of the military in politics at various junctures of institutional changes in Myanmar (i.e. in 1948, 1958, 1962, and 1988) (Steinberg 1981; 1982; Silverstein 1977; 2004; Smith 1999; Fink 2001; Taylor 1998; Carey 1997; Callahan 2001). The modern military in Myanmar began as part of the independence struggle in the 1930s. On the eve of World War II, the Myanmar army was more an embodiment of British colonial attitudes than of Burmese reality. Until the 1930s, British policy excluded Burmans from the armed forces (Steinberg 1981: 12). By keeping the ethnic minorities in the hills and the people in the plains divided, it was easier for the Britishers to maintain control (Fink 2001: 18). In 1940, the Thakins, the political movement of the students and young intelligentsia, secretly sent one of their leaders, Aung San, to China to seek aid for their revolt (Silverstein 2004). Picked up by the Japanese in Amoy, he was taken to Tokyo. There he met leaders of the Japanese Army command who were aware of the independence aspirations of the Thakins. Aung San entered into an agreement with them. It was agreed that Japan would help Myanmar to gain her independence by supplying her with necessary arms. At the same time, an underground revolutionary movement began to form inside Myanmar in preparation for the anticipated uprising against the British.

Aung San returned in 1941 and recruited twenty-nine Burmans to go secretly with him to Hainan Island where they would be given military training by the Japanese. These 'Thirty Heroes' formed the nucleus of the Burma Independence Army (BIA) (Fink 2001: 21). The army, thus, organised was a "political force first and a military force, second—the officer corps seeing themselves as freedom fighters, not professional soldiers" (Taylor 1998: 6). When the Pacific War broke out, they returned to Thailand, recruited the first members of the Burma Independence Army and followed the Japanese into Myanmar. Some of their units fought the British and the experience gave them pride and confidence.

During the four years of occupation, the Japanese did not succeed either in bringing the whole of Myanmar under their control or in winning the universal support of the people. Faced with harassing tactics by the Allies and the threat of invasion, the Japanese tried to gain support from the Burmese only by promises of freedom (Silverstein 1977: 16). During the war, the army's name was changed, first to the Burma Defence Army (BDA) in 1942, then the Burma National Army (BNA) and at wars end in 1943, to the Patriotic Burmese Forces. On 27 March 1945, it revolted against the Japanese and joined with the Allies in their final phase of the war against the Japanese (Steinberg 1981: 13).

During the Japanese occupation, many Burmese acquired administrative experience by filling important positions in the government. When Japan allowed Myanmar to proclaim independence on August 1, 1943, a government headed by Ba Maw was permitted to take charge of most of the administrative apparatus under the supervision of the colonial masters (Silverstein 1977: 17). In this period of nominal independence, an anti-Japanese resistance movement arose under the direction of the Anti-Fascist People's Freedom League—AFPFL—whose leadership included a number of Burmese who had been cooperating with the Japanese. The AFPFL opened its ranks to all the people of Myanmar regardless of ethnic group, religion or political belief and after the war it emerged as the most important voice in Burmese politics. It was an anti-fascist organisation which included the Communist Party, the Socialist Party and independent nationalists (Gravers 1999: 51). Aung San was the leader of the AFPFL and was not aligned to the parties which established the league. The Communists were however, excluded from the AFPFL in 1946 on account of their unwillingness to promote a negotiated settlement with the British (*ibid.*).

The negotiation of independence was hurried and carried out against the background of sudden collapse of British power in India and the beginning of the Cold War (Horton 2005: 112). A meeting between British Prime Minister Clement Atlee and Aung San took place in London in January 1947. Although no exact timetable was laid down, the agreement set out the course of events leading up to Myanmar's independence. In April, elections were to be held to a Constituent Assembly to determine the future of the Constitution. Until the transfer of power, the Governor's Executive Council was to act as the interim government in Myanmar (Smith 1999: 78).

In order to solve the problems of the frontier areas, in between the 'January Agreement' and April elections, Panglong Conference took place in February 1947 (as discussed earlier) (Smith 1999; Diller 1993; Fink 2001; Gravers 1999; Silverstein 1977). On the basis of this agreement, the principle for the formation of new Myanmar was agreed. Under the Agreement, the Shans, Kachins, and Chins were to cooperate with the interim Burmese government in framing the constitution on the condition that they receive full autonomy in internal administration and enjoy all the rights and privileges regarded as fundamental in democratic countries (Diller 1993: 395). The Kachins agreed to have the question of an autonomous Kachin State considered further by the Constituent Assembly to be elected. The concept of a federal union was agreed upon, and ethnic states were to be created with full autonomy over their internal affairs (Fink 2001: 22).

Although the conference agreed to cooperate on the political freedom of internal administration amongst the minorities, and Aung San promised to secure cultural and democratic rights for the ethnic groups, there were, however, several shortcomings (Gravers 1999: 49). Only four representatives of the Karens attented the Conference as an observer and did not took part in the proceedings. The Mon and Arakanese from ministerial Burma and Pao and Wa from Frontier Areas were also not represented (Smith 1999: 79). The inadequacies of the agreement reached at Panglong became apparent with independence. The general terms of the Agreement resurfaced in the Constituent Assembly debates and ultimately in the Constitution adopted on 24 September 1947. However, the Conference also confirmed the ethnic difference, and when independence came in 1948 the inconsistencies in the different conceptions of national identity and political union were brought sharply and implacably into focus (Gravers 1999: 49). A final settlement between Nu and British Prime Minister Clement Atlee was signed on October 17, 1947. This agreement provided that Myanmar would become a fully sovereign and independent state outside the Commonwealth. The agreement was ratified by the Brirish Parliament in December and Myanmar became independent on January 4, 1948 (Silverstein 1977: 21).

However, with the assassination of Aung San, the stage was set for Myanmar's tragedy. Myanmar lost the politician who most clearly understood the dangers of making ethnicity and religion the cornerstone of nationalism and of incorporating this mixture in the state apparatus (Gravers 1999: 49). The Panglong agreement was never fully honoured: the crucial clause five, guaranteeing full autonomy in internal administration, was omitted from the text (Horton 2005: 112). In the Constitution there was no mention of the term 'federal' or 'federalism', however, this was its main intention. Discussions leading to promises made by the Burman leaders to the minorities resulted in the creation of a unique federal union, which was more unitary than federal, and led to most Karens and Karennis rejecting it (Silverstein 2004). The 1947 Constitution formed a multi-party bicameral parliamentary democracy. Although the new Constitution recognized the rights of the ethnic minorities it, nevertheless, emphasized on a single centralized government (Diller 1993: 395).

The Shan State was to be reconstituted as one, with the extraordinary right of secession after a ten year trial period. Karrenni states were similarly to be reconstituted as one with the same right of secession. Kachin, however, abandoned this right in return for the inclusion in the new Kachin State of the two major towns of Myitkyino and Bhamo. The Chins, who were politically quiescent ended up without even a State, instead they were formed into a special division (Smith 1999: 80; Diller 1993: 395; Fink 2001: 22-23). The final designation and status of a Karen territory and political rights were left to be decided after independence, while the Mon and Arakanese of the Ministerial Burma received no distinctive recognition at all. Thus, as the Constitution drafting took place, groups of Karens, Karennis, Mons, Buddhist Arakanese and Muslims in Arakan territory began preparing for armed struggle. In fact, the failure to resolve adequately the demands of the ethnic nationalities during the constitutional drafting process set the conditions for the outbreak of the violence later (for details see Article 201-206, Constitution of Burma, 1947) (Fink 2001: 23). The document also contained guarantees for the democratic rights of all citizens, irrespective of race, birth, religion and sex. Heavily influenced by Socialism, the constitution also established a welfare state providing for individual rights to education, employment, health care, and support for the aged (Diller 1993: 395).

Myanmar at the cusp of independence had an uncertain future and was caught in the chaos as political rivals took up arms to advance their claim to power (Taylor 2005: 15). During the first decade (1948-1958), an enduring insurrection kept the country in a state of semi-war. There were particularly, three groups which could be identified—the Communists, Peoples' Voluntary Organisation (PVO), Karen National Defense Organisation (KNDO) (Silverstein 1977: 26).

Peoples Volunteer Organisation (PVO) was formed by Aung San from the Burman soldiers who were not taken into the new army, as a home guard to help maintain law and order in the countryside (Fink 2001: 23). But its real mission was political: to give the AFPFL a vehicle by which to intimidate the colonial rulers in the growing struggle for independence (Silverstein 2004). Such forces existed in the 1930s and were nothing new for Myanmar. Since, the PVO members shared the ideas and values of and had close personal ties to the leaders and men in the new army and the rival political parties in and out of the AFPFL—the socialists and communists—doubts were raised in many minds as to whether there was a real separation between the professional army, the political army and the parties. So long as Aung San lived, the PVO remained united and loyal to him and the AFPFL. Aung San's assassination in 1947 left the PVO leaderless and subject to the persuasions of rival political groups seeking to lead the nation (Gravers 1999: 51-52).

The Communists initiated revolt on 28 March 1948 to institute a 'Communist State' through an armed revolution. During this time, the PVO split and the dissent group joined the Communists in revolt (Fink 2001: 24; Silverstein 1977: 26; Gravers 1999: 52). The army also began to come apart. Thus, when the Communist Party went into revolt, less than three months after independence, divisive forces began operative. The 1st and 3rd Burma Rifles—two Burman battalions—deserted with their weapons and joined forces with the revolutionaries. Significantly, the fourth Burma Rifle, commanded by Brigadier Ne Win remained loyal to the government (Gravers 1999: 52). Following independence and the failure of the Constituent Assembly to solve the problem of the Karens' place in the new union, communal violence erupted between Burmans and Karens (Silverstein 2004). In January 1949, the Karen Forces under the banner Karen National Defense Organization (KNDO) rebelled. As the violence increased, three battalions of Karen Rifles deserted and joined the KNDO. This was a major crisis for military leadership in Myanmar (Steinberg 1981: 13). Meanwhile, the remnants of the Chiang Kai-Sheikh's KMT had fled and taken refuge in Myanmar. They sought to join the indigenous rebels in the Shan State, and thereby posed a new threat to the 'Union'.

When the diplomatic initiatives to end the KMT build up and to appease Beijing failed, the Burmese government sent the army to the troubled region. The army established a military administration in this region and soon embarked on a massive transformation of the armed forces (Callahan 2001: 417). By 1950, their (KMT forces) numbers grew to around 12,000. They became a major concern for the Burmese political and army leadership when the KMT forces started receiving airdrops of US supplied arms over the next few years. The KMT threats were not really laid to rest until 1961 (Smith 1999: 155-57).

By 1958, the insurgents appeared to have become demoralised and many responded to government's offer to leave the jungle, lay down their weapons and rejoin society. These measures, however, did not bring peace to the countryside (Silverstein 1977: 27). Shan youths with the help of the Shan dissident leader took arms to fight for greater political autonomy. Similar rebellious activity developed among Kachins, increasing the danger of the existing insurgencies and posing a serious threat to the nation's unity (Fink 2001: 24).

3.1.1 Parliamentary Democracy

The structure of the government adopted after independence followed the British parliamentary model. A primary goal of the founders of independent Myanmar was to create a government blending the values and ideas of liberal democracy inherited from the British with the socialist values and goals expressed in Western Socialism (Silverstein 1977: 54-55). The leaders of the post-independent Myanmar embraced parliamentary democracy as the principal political system, but continued their fascination with socialistic principles as a basis for equitable economic development. The political system exhibited competitive party politics in a democratic setting; state intervention in the economic system was characterised by an indigeneous interpretation of economic nationalism with socialistic leanings (Than 2007: 49). The Constitution also sought to solve the major problem facing the nation of constructing an Union in which formerly separate people could join together so as to benefit from unity, while retaining a nominal degree of autonomy (Smith 1999: 27). The Anti-Fascist People's Freedom League (AFPFL) dominated Myanmar's politics for more than a decade after independence. The machinery of government and party overlapped to such an extent that the two seemed to be indistinguishable at times.

The parliamentary political system installed by the AFPFL government at the time of independence had encouraged competition and divisiveness among the political elite of the country (Taylor 2005: 16). After independence, various political groups within ruling AFPFL argued over their differences more frequently, by vigorously pushing the party to adopt their preferred policies and to appoint their members to top party and government positions. As a result of this internal turmoil, within first year after independence, the AFPFL government found itself being paralysed by factional and power struggles (Hlaing 2008: 151).

The idea that the opposition could play a constructive role in putting up different points of view had 'no roots in Burma'. It had always been understood as insubordination, and leaders in 1950s found it difficult to negotiate and work together with political representatives from other factions and parties (Fink 2001: 25). As the wave of insurgency subsided, members and supporters of the ruling party struggled for power and privileges. Patronage was widespread with AFPFL and power became personalised. These shortcomings aggravated the centrifugal tendencies brought about by personal rivalries among the ruling elite and led to a decline in the AFPFL's popularity (Than 2007: 51).

After the poor performance in the 1956 elections, League's cohesion began to weaken. The inner party rivalry continued despite a public display of unity among its leaders. Although the AFPFL continued to dominate the Parliament, yet it split into two antagonistic groups in April 1958— 'Clean' and the 'Stable' AFPFL (Smith 1999: 176; Hlaing 2008: 155; Silverstein 1977: 28; Fink 2001: 27; Steinberg 1981: 15). Ideology played little or no role in the split, as all were committed to vague socialist goals. Issues revolved around personalities and cliques. Both the groups wanted to retain the official name of the AFPFL, the pre-eminent political designation since 1945 (Steinberg 1981: 15).

After months of accusations and revelations of corruption and crime, U Nu sought to end the dispute by calling a special session of Parliament and letting it decide, which faction would govern. He was able to hold on to power with the help of the National United Front (NUF) and the representatives of the minorities (Silverstein 1977: 28). The resulting unstable political situation led to widespread unrest and confusion. In August, as the situation deteriorated, the curse of Burmese politics continued to spread. The air was filled with coups and assassination attempts. The matters went out of control by September 1958 (Smith 1999: 177-78). Unwilling to face the regular sessions of the Parliament, U Nu turned to General Ne Win and relinquished his position as commander-in-chief of the armed forces to General Win. He in turn agreed that the military would hold a free and fair election within six months. However, with Parliamentary approval, General Ne Win extended the tenure of his caretaker government from 6 to 18 months (Hlaing 2008: 155). U Nu, announced that the handover had been voluntary, but in reality he was left with no choice in the matter. In anticipation of the impending crisis, the military had surrounded Rangoon. U Nu was, in fact, faced with a coup if he did not act. The coup was characterized as a 'coup by consent' and a 'pseudo-constitutional-peaceful-military coup-d'etat' (quoted in Steinberg 1981: 16). At that stage, according to Steinberg (1981: 16), "U Nu took the constitutional way out, Ne Win the constitutional way in". The takeover was a positive military response to the U Nu's request to the army to bring about conditions that would allow the peaceful and non-partisan holding of elections.

3.1.2 Caretaker Government

Under the caretaker government, which was also known as Bogyoke (General's) Government, Ne Win achieved several successes (Fink 2001: 27). There were three main objectives of military control—to re-establish law and order, to combat economic insurgents, and to prepare for civilian elections

(Steinberg 1981: 16). On the eve of the formation of the caretaker government the military leaders held a conference at which they defined the national ideology, as they understood it, and their role in upholding it, declaring that so long as their strength remained, 'the Constitution shall remain inviolate'. They held that the nation's goal was to build a political-economic system on the principles of justice, liberty and equality and to construct a democratic society based on socialist economy. In the 'National Ideology and the Role of Defense Services', published 1960, three main objectives were set out: the restoration of peace and rule of law; the consolidation of democracy; and the establishment of a socialist economy (Silverstein 1977: 77; Smith 1999: 179). They pledged to pursue the aims of national politics as distinct from party politics. The caretaker government gave Ne Win a chance to put the army's ideology and theories into practice; and as discussed earlier, while he followed the letter of the constitution, he violated its spirit (Silverstein 2004).

The military caretaker government sought to clean up the cities which were filled with squatters. Huts lined-up throughout the thoroughfares and covered vacant lots (Fink 2001: 27; Silverstein 1977: 28; Steinberg 1981: 20; Smith 1999: 179). Ne Win kept the food prices low and moved the squatter communities to newly established satellite towns (Fink 2001: 27). The economic activities of the military caretaker government were of greatest importance because of the attitudes they created within the military. The Defense Services Institute (DSI) was vastly expanded. Its main objective was development of national economy; lowering of prices; expansion into new economic fields and propagation of the industrial and commercial knowledge. The military further perceived DSI to play a significant part in the process of Burmanisation (Steinberg 1981: 17-18).

The military caretaker administration's most important legacy was the continued development of a national political identity for the tatmadaw under General Ne Win (Smith 1999: 179). In its effort to deal more effectively with insurgency and lawlessness in the countryside, the caretaker government formed security and administrative committees composed of representatives from the army, police and administration to coordinate and cooperate in establishing or restoring law and order. The Frontier Areas Administration assumed direct jurisdiction over remote border areas and took responsibility for security and improvement in services to the people in those areas. As a result of these changes a more centralised administration developed throughout the nation, and internal security was improved (Silverstein 1977: 78). The caretaker government, further, led to the integration of the frontier areas and local chiefs with the Union. The government brought pressure on the chiefs in the Shan and Kayah States to surrender their historic rights and transfer administration to elected leaders (Fink 2001: 27-28). A constitutional amendment, passed in 1959 confirmed these changes and was hailed as an important step in the democratisation of the frontier areas. But the change did not bring peace to these troubled states. The destruction of the traditional political and economic hierarchy has been a factor in increasing Shan state resistance to the Union Government (Steinberg 1981: 18).

In the caretaker government, AFPFL—Stable formed the key component of the military (Hlaing 2008: 155). General Ne Win complied with the election date which was set for February 1960. The military leaders hoped to influence the outcome of the election and the AFPFL—Stable faction flaunted their connection with the high ranking officers (Fink 2001: 28). Backed by senior military leaders, the AFPFL—Stable leaders appeared confident of their electoral victory. They believed that their supporters in the military would do everything to undermine the position of the AFPFL—Clean in the election. The outcome of the election was, however, contrary to the expectations of the AFPFL—Stable because a large number of people, especially, the business elite, who suffered due to caretaker government's regulatory measures were dissatisfied and acted on this animosity by whole heartedly supporting the AFPFL—Clean (Hlaing 2008: 155). Thus, when the third national election was held in February

1960, the Clean AFPFL won an overwhelming majority—203 out of 250 seats.

After the elections, in a third governmental change, the military transferred power back to the winning party—AFPFL—Clean, which was renamed as Pyidaungsu or Union Party. The new government under the leadership of U Nu called for strengthening of democratic institutions; establishment of Buddhism as the state religion; creation of new state for Mons and Arakanese within the Union; and development of a plan for promoting social and economic growth (Silverstein 1977: 29). Yet, despite its popular mandate Union Party government could last for just two years. The triumphant return of U Nu to office precipitated events that demonstrated the faults in the Burmese democracy (Steinberg 1981: 20). These faults were well articulated by the military during the caretaker government period.

A major cause was the continued failure of a truly democratic, multi-party system of government to take root (Smith 1999: 187). Factionalism within the Union Government was, in fact, conceived and given life in the new Pyidaungsu government. Three different factions were created—Thakin group, U group and the Bo group (Hlaing 2008: 156). As the tension between these three groups intensified, party leadership had torn AFPFL apart before (Smith 1999: 187). Continuing economic and administrative stagnation seemed to grip the state as U Nu began to carry out his campaign promises. He tried to appease the Buddhists by making Buddhism the state religion. Further, by espousing a constitutional amendment allowing freedom of religion, he to some extent appeased the Christians. Minorities and ethnic communities, on the other hand, remained unrelieved under the limited autonomy and insufficient economic progress and rewards (Steinberg 1981: 20). The secessionist movement among the Shans and discontent among the other minorities came to dominate the relations between the State and the Union Governments (Silverstein 1977: 29). On the question of re-establishing harmony among the people of Myanmar, especially Shans, Kachins and Burmans, the government hoped that a final settlement could be worked out at a federal seminar held in February and March 1962, but as a result of the military coup it was dissolved before it could complete its negotiations (*ibid.*). On the whole, the deficiencies in the quality and personnel of the Pyidaungsu administration and government's failure to resolve the urgent problems of the day caused U Nu's ultimate downfall (Smith 1999: 187).

Military under the command of General Ne Win witnessed significant changes. The government authorised the recruitment of PVOs loyal to the state, and other former World War II soldiers to form territorial units (Sitwundans) to buttress the depleted army. Under Ne Win's leadership, a process of Burman domination in the army began. Despite the loyal support given by Kachin, Chin and Shan battalions, their units gradually were reformed with Burman officers in command and Burman soldiers in their ranks. Aung San's federated army gave way to Ne Win's Burman-dominated and integrated army (Silverstein 2004). The new army became more professional with the establishment of a military academy in 1954, and later a National Defence College.

3.1.3 Establishment of Military Rule: 1962-74

In the wake of the Federal Seminar in February-March 1962 in which leaders were allowed to put up their case so as to examine various alternative solutions advocated by the participants, that the Parliamentary democracy ultimately collapsed (Smith 1999: 196; Fink 2001: 29; Silverstein 1977: 30; Steinberg 1981: 22-23). The military under General Ne Win organised a bloodless coup on March 2, 1962. A seventeen member Revolutionary Council was established—consisting of all the members from the military (Steinberg 1981: 22-23). The coup suspended the Constitution, dissolved the Parliament, abolished the state councils and took control over the state. Although the causes of the coup have been subject to considerable speculation, Brigadier Aung Gyi, the main spokesman of the Revolutionary Council made it explicit by stating—"We had economic, religious and political crisis with the issue of federalism as the most important reason for the coup" (quoted in Smith 1999: 196; Silverstein 1977: 30).

The Revolutionary Council led by General Ne Win, which came to power in the wake of the coup attempted to carry out fundamental structural transformations in the country's political and economic affairs by forming the Burma Socialist Programme party—BSPP and adopting the Burmese Way to Socialism (Hlaing 2008: 157). From the outset, the military displaced the institutions created at independence, replaced the civilian leadership with members of their own organisation, and substituted their thought for that of their political predecessors. The Constitution was suspended and became inoperative in areas where the Revolutionary Council, the military governing body, issued decrees and promulgated orders. The courts were reconstituted (Steinberg 1981: 23). Old parties were outlawed and replaced by the military's own new party, the BSPP, the only political party allowed after 1964. Freedom of press eventually was restricted and replaced by an official publication, the Working Peoples Daily. Most of all, the federal system, while remaining in name, in fact, became a centralised administrative system. Security Administration Councils, composed of representatives from the army, civil service and police, replaced state political and administrative organs (Silverstein 2004). The new system was organised hierarchically with control located in Rangoon.

Ne Win's vehicle of reform, the BSPP, was announced in July 1962 and military's new ideology was contained in two major policy statements published during the first year of military government—the Burmese Way to Socialism and the System of Correlation of Man and his Environment (elaborated in the next section). Through his Revolutionary Council, General Ne Win sought to remake Burmese politics and society. Land and wealth were to be redistributed, foreigners stripped of their assets, and self-serving politicians and capitalists replaced with loyal army men dedicated to serving the nation. The army ensured its political control of the country by establishing 'security and administrative councils' led by military officers (Smith 1999: 199). General Ne Win started by replacing approximately 2000 civilian members of the country's administration with military personnel and security councils were set up at the divisional, township, and village level (Fink 2001: 32). As BSPP slowly began to evolve, even the BSPP's administrative wings were set up to run parallel to the divisions of the military command.

The military was also able to extend its control over the national economy and the Defense Services Institute (DSI) became the major commercial institution of the country involved in shipping, banking, construction, transport and a variety of other business services. By 1963, all banking, importing and exporting, production and distribution sectors were nationalised (Silverstein 1977: 33). This state led development without adequate preparations ruined the economy. By 1967, there were widespread shortage of rice, cooking oil and other basic commodities. As a consequence black marketing and corruption became rampant (Steinberg 1981: 37).

State-led socialist development in Myanmar was largely influenced by ideas and notions closely associated with socialism and economic nationalism endured during the pre-colonial period (Than 2007). These manifestations of 'reactive nationalism' against the colonial power continued after independence and dominated the political landscape by the '1945 generation' of political and military leaders whose credentials were legitimated by their role in the 'anti-fascist revolution' of 1945 (*ibid.*). Historically, it was also the result of the economic experience and alienation of the population from the sources of societal control. Socialism along with nationalism was also nurtured with Buddhist traditions. Buddhism, in fact, acquired a new vigour and a more pronounced role because of its close association with both nationalism and socialism (Steinberg 1982: 35). The intermingling of Socialism, Nationalism and Buddhism in 'Burmese Way to Socialism' disguised the military foundations of Ne Win (Based on interview with. Zaw Aun Win).[1]

All institutions that could challenge the Revolutionary Council were dismantled or neutralised while potential dissidents and pressure groups were either co-opted or emasculated through socio-economic and administrative controls (Than 2007: 112). Mass rallies and support for the Revolutionary Council was more like a ritual deliberately organised to disguise the real character of the politics which was of an exclusionary type. The Burmese Way to Socialism failed both to improve the economy and to gain real support amongst the people. By the end of the decade, Ne Win and his co-leaders gradually shifted to a new direction.

By 1971, the BSPP was converted from a cadre to a mass party. Military rulers ordered the BSPP to begin planning for a constitutional form of government. It, therefore, started working for a new constitution (Silverstein 1977: 35). Despite changes in structure, the party remained a political vehicle for the military with General Ne Win as its head and senior military officers monopolizing all sub-leadership posts. In April 1972, while the party pursued its tasks, Ne Win and nineteen senior military officers retired from the Defence Services. At the same time the government changed its name from the Revolutionary Council to the 'Government of Burma'. Ne Win remained Prime Minister and most of the same senior military leaders, thereafter retired, continued as government heads; four civilian cabinet officers were added to their ranks. During this period, Ne Win abolished the Secretariat inherited from the British colonial system, and transferred its responsibilities to the ministers. In terms of who led the nation, these changes were more nominal than real as the military retained near exclusive control of power. A new constitution was approved by the people in a referendum in December 1973 (Than 2007: 112). Early in 1974, elections were held to fill the seats in the National Assembly. Subsequently, the military rule entered its second phase—'Constitutional Dictatorship' in which Ne Win and his military officers continued to rule under a Constitution that legally concentrated all powers in the hands of the BSPP (Silverstein 1977: 35).

3.1.4 Constitutional Dictatorship: BSPP Rule: 1974-88

In March 1974, the second phase of military rule began. On March 2, 1974, the twelfth anniversary of the military coup, the Revolutionary Council dissolved itself, and the new government was officially installed (Steinberg 1981: 65). The constitution institutionalised the power of the BSPP. It was directed to lead the nation; no other parties were allowed (Silverstein 2004). The 'Preamble' of the Constitution provides a prime position for the BSPP. It specifically lays down "We, the working people, firmly resolved that we shall faithfully follow the leadership of the Burma Socialist Programme Party". According to Article 11 of the Constitution, "The State shall adopt a single-party system. The Burma Socialist Programme Party is the sole political party and it shall lead the State". The party was charged specifically with the responsibility of drawing up lists of candidates for all offices in consultation with its own mass and class organisations and the electorate (Article 179). The party was also empowered to give advice and suggestions to government at all levels on economic planning, the annual budget, and anything else it chooses to discuss (Article 205). Like the army, government was centralised and hierarchical. The various levels of administration were tied together by the principle of democratic centralism.

The new Constitution codified changes in the military structure related to reorganisation of the administrative structure. According to Article 29(b) of the Constitution, "The different levels of administrative areas of the Socialist Republic of the Union of Burma shall be as follows: (1) wards or village-tracts; (2) townships; (3) states or divisions; (4) the State. Hence, the lowest administrative level in rural areas was the village tract, a grouping together of several villages for administrative purposes. In urban areas, its equivalent was the ward. The next higher level was of township followed by division or state. At the apex of the system was the Pyithu Hluttaw—Peoples' Assembly, the titular source of all power in the state" (Steinberg 1981: 69-70). At each of these levels a Peoples' Council was formed which composed of ten to thirty members. Electoral representation at each of these levels was based on BSPP's prerogative of nominating official candidates. Elections, therefore, implied confirmation rather than competition (Than 2007: 161).

Once the euphoria of the constitutional government passed, Peoples' Assembly devoted its time to the major questions inherited from the military government—security, national unity and economic improvement. Ne Win gave a speech on the differences between the two governments he headed. According to him, "under the new government Peoples' Assembly is the source of authority, with the people granted power and encouraged to act with self-reliance and independence. In the present one-party system, according to him, there was no longer need for inter-party strife and struggle for power in the legislature" (quoted in Silverstein 1977: 139). But moralising and lecturing was no answer to the immediate problems of insurgency, national unity and economic decay. The ailing economy, continuing insurgency, thriving black-market and narcotics traffic were some of the major problems that have plagued the Ne Win regime for a greater part of its 26 year life span (Gyi 1983: 225). These problems were inextricably intertwined, but the economy and insurgency were the main issues out of which grew the other two.

Insurgency, which began during the first constitutional period and continued into the military period, remained an important fact of life for the leaders of the new constitutional dictatorship (Fink 2001: 47-48; Smith 1999: 198-354). The problems facing the new government do not come only from the insurgents. The failures of the military such as mal-administration, black-marketing, inefficient management, and corruption among both civilian and military officials, were as much a part of the new as they were of the old (Silverstein 1977: 140). Both the Revolutionary Council and its constitutional successor could not solve the problem of the inefficiency of the state managed economy. It, in fact, became a source of financing state's enemies and creating a self-perpetuating series of conflict (Taylor 2005: 17).

The implementation of the new Constitution in 1974 brought no substantial change to Myanmar's economy. Production of basic goods was less than planned and what entered the market was not distributed well, resulting in higher prices, hoarding, black markets and outright shortages (Silverstein 1977: 141, 164). As the state's economic drive deteriorated in the mid-1980s, inflation and shortage of consumer goods brought economic hardship to the populace (Than 2007: 164). National economic performance fell into complete disarray, inflation was uncontrollably high, the manufactured sector showed a negative growth rate and exports and imports dropped to record lows (Hlaing 2008: 161).

Although there were institutional restructuring and limited reforms during the mid-1970s, in reality it turned out to be dysfunctional. Economic stagnation became deep rooted in the seventies (Alamgir 1997: 343). The post-1974 monetary and fiscal policies were aimed at controlling price inflation, financing state led economic development, and maintaining a favourable balance of payments position. In reality, the financial sector remained undeveloped and the government was unable to prevent persistent budget deficits and recurring balance of payments problems brought about by poor resource mobilisation and export stagnation (Than 2007: 179, 200). Scarce foreign exchange was tightly controlled and centralised. "Constraints such as weak demand, backward technology, poor infrastructure, inelastic pricing, over-valued exchange rate, over centralisation, over concentration on a few commodities, bad weather, population pressure, inhibited export growth" (*ibid.*: 201). Another aspect of Myanmar's external trade was the so-called informal trade that had considerable impact on the overall economy due to its wide scope and huge magnitude. The cross-border black market not only deprived the state of substantial tax revenues and trading profits but also undermined its authority in terms of the flouting of socialist principles.

Monetary and fiscal reforms were marred by the drastic demonetisation measures taken in November 1985, in which roughly one-quarter of the currency was taken out of circulation, which included 20, 50 and 100 kyat notes. This action was more a politically inspired punitive measure than an effective monetary instrument to rectify the problem of excess liquidity and illegal trading (Than 2007: 193). Thereafter, the money supply continued to grow a pace and the state again resorted to demonetisation on September 5, 1987. About 56 per cent of the currency was invalidated, which included 25, 35 and 75 kyat banknotes. Both legal and illegal businesses were affected (Taylor 2055: 20).

All the measures of the Socialist government to remedy the economic problems only worsened the country's economic situation and further contributed to the outbreak of social unrest in many parts of the country (Hlaing 2008: 162). In May-June 1974, a major strike led by workers broke out over food shortages, rising prices, and bad labour conditions. This erupted at the railway workshop in Insein and spread quickly to other state concerns. As rioting continued, troops were called out to restore order and over hundred were arrested and imprisoned (Silverstein 1977: 141). Universities, colleges and educational institutions were closed to prevent further demonstration.

In December 1974, the society exploded once again, this time over the manner in which the government sought to deny any honours to UN Secretary General U Thant, when his body was returned to Myanmar for burial. Because of the long-standing political feud between U Thant and Ne Win, the Myanmar government sent no official delegation to receive the coffin (Fink 2001: 43). The students discontented with an appropriate ceremony and inadequate burial site for U Thant, seized his body in a clear protest against the military. Along with the monks, they attempted to bury it at a former student union building before its destruction by Ne Win in 1962 (Steinberg 1981: 73). The government responded by declaring martial law and sending troops to the campus. They were successful in reclaiming the coffin and reburying it at a cemetery near Shwedagon Pagoda.

In June 1975, a year after the workers strike, both students and workers held a joint demonstration marking the anniversary of 1974 workers strike. As they marched down, more and more people joined the protest (Fink 2001: 44). Sit-down strikes, labour demonstrations and other forms of protest by workers and students lasted for one week. The government subsequently resorted to force to break-up and end the demonstrations (Silverstein 1977: 143). Again the government closed all the universities and educational institutions and they were not to open until January 1976.

On March 6, 1976, yet another demonstration took place, although it was less widespread. It was organised to mark the anniversary of a prominent left-wing leader, Thakin Kodaw Hmaing. In anticipation that the crowd may become rampant, the universities and institutes were closed (Steinberg 1981: 73; Fink 2001: 44; Silverstein 1977: 143). Over more than hundred students were arrested in Rangoon itself and sentenced to an imprisonment ranging from five to fifteen years.

Although the *modus operandi* of the BSPP professed the guidelines of 'inner-party democracy' and 'democratic centralism', according to Than (2007: 163), in reality it was centralism which prevailed over 'democracy'. This led to authoritarian practices and rigidities. The centrality of the idea of the party as a political force insulated the BSPP from the socio-economic and political changes occurring beyond the arena of routinised political exercises (*ibid.*). The state also lost the ability to reform itself and the economy because of the political necessity to protect a large number of unproductive positions in the bureaucracy, party and state-owned industries. Moreover, the leadership of the BSPP and the bureaucracy came increasingly to be filled by less competent army officers. As a part of the patronising policy of Ne Win, many competent officers were eased out of office or demoted because of their inability to conform to the norms of the system (Taylor 2005: 17-18). Antagonism between those who remained in armed forces and those who remained in party also grew. As a part of the attempt to raise fund and recruit the loyalists, several small economic enterprises were established such as bee farming centres, small food processing factories, orchid plantations, and chicken farms (Hlaing 2008: 160). This style of administration threatened the legitimacy and continuation of the regime. The riots and demonstrations were strong warnings to the party leadership that something very basic was wrong with the system (Silverstein 1977: 144).

The system remained intact, with relatively little change until 1988. The first sign of real change came in August 1987, when Ne Win startled the nation by admitting 'failure and faults' in the management of the economy and called for open discussion about the past and change (Silverstein 2004). On August 10, Ne Win made a speech to senior party and government officials. "Noting that the system over which he presided for twenty-five years was increasingly incapable and that the world and domestic economic and political conditions had changed since the army took power in 1962 and the new Constitution adopted in 1974. Therefore, he suggested that the existing political order was in need of revision" (quoted in Taylor 2005: 20). Prospects for further change in the economy and politics were promised by Ne Win in a subsequent speech in October. The regime had publicly admitted that the socialist revolution introduced in 1962 had been a failure and the general populace was losing faith it had in the credibility of the regime.

The ultimate collapse of the BSPP took seven months, from March to September 1988 in a series of event. For several months reports of student-led protests over shortages of essential commodities and spiraling rice prices had been circulating. But it was only in March of that year, that the world first took note of their growing momentum (Smith 1999: 2). As students took to streets in protest, the government replied severely. They clamped down with horrifying force and an estimate 100 civilians were killed. Although the demonstrations subsided as a result of the army's crackdown and abrupt closure of the colleges and universities, the protests resumed soon after the campuses were opened in early June. In the demonstrations that followed, students were joined by monks, workers and high school students. As the clashes broke out, this time, the security forces opened fire and several demonstrators were killed (*ibid.*: 3). Throughout the month of June rioting continued and there were reports of gatherings and protests in Rangoon, Mandalay, Moulmein, Taunggyi, Pegu and a number of provincial towns.

Developments came to a climax in July 1988 while the nation was in turmoil. Government's crackdown worsened the situation. Protests against shortages of supplies in the shops and rising prices of the essential goods such as cooking oil and medicine continued to rise high dramatically. In the midst of this worsening backdrop, the BSPP announced its emergency Congress. At this emergency session, Ne Win announced his resignation as party head and urged the leaders to consider the creation of a multiparty system, among other changes. The resulting change in leadership from Ne Win to Sein Lwin aggravated the deeply deteriorating legitimacy of the BSPP and the State leadership (Than 2007: 164). Subsequently, the elaborate political and administrative superstructure collapsed.

Although the party permitted Ne Win to resign, it did not adopt his recommendations. Instead, it appointed as its new leader General Sein Lwin, another protégé of Ne Win. He had the reputation of having led his military unit in suppressing dissent on the university campus in 1962, and again in 1974 where hundreds of students were killed and wounded. In response to his appointment, people flooded back on the streets. People's main target was the hated Sein Lwin, who had been dubbed as the 'butcher of Rangoon' (Smith 1999: 4). To bring matter under control, martial law was declared on August 3 and was immediately followed by the call for a general strike.

A new mass demonstration was called by the students for the auspiciously chosen '8-8-88'. Across the country, workers laid down tools and took to the streets. This time, the government's crackdown was most draconian. Shootings were reported in many towns and cities across the country. To put down the growing national unrest, which had been building up during the year Sein Lwin ordered the military to suppress the strike of unarmed civilians; it resulted in the death of thousands (Silverstein 2004). On August 12, after a brief but bloody interregnum of just 18 days, Sein Lwin resigned and his place was taken over by Dr. Maung Maung, who was the only non-military man ever to have served in the higher ranks of the BSPP.

The "8888 Uprising", the largest ever national Burmese uprising demanding democracy ended on 18 September 1988. The student leaders promoted a 'set of ten demands' for the restoration of a democratic government in Myanmar. At this critical juncture, when the people felt that they were on the verge of victory, General Saw Maung, the head of the army and very much a loyal subordinate of Ne Win and his protégé Sein Lwin, organised a coup and on September 18 seized power and ordered the armed forces to suppress all dissent (Smith 1999: 15). The BSPP government fell and the military imposed martial law giving absolute power to the commander-in-chief, General Saw Maung, in order to quash the demonstrations. The army established as a government in the form of State Law and Order Restoration Council (SLORC) (Taylor 2005: 21). This resulted in abandonment of Burmese Way to Socialism and the eventual dissolution of the BSPP. Thus, the military's carefully constructed constitutional dictatorship crumbled and the army found it necessary to abandon the facade of constitutional government in favour of naked power to restore its leadership (Silverstein 2004).

3.1.5 Military Junta: SLORC 1988-97

On September 18, 1988, General Saw Maung Commander of Burma Army carried out a coup in support of a tottering military government. Battered by widespread popular riots that had evolved over the previous months into a peoples' revolution, the government was under popular siege (Steinberg 2001: 2). Brutal suppression of popular discontent followed the coup. The military instituted a new government called the State Law and Order Restoration Council (SLORC). It re-instituted the old name of the state, the "Union of Burma" dropping its previous socialist appellation, "the Socialist Republic of the Union of Burma". It dissolved the previous single legal party—BSPP—and reconstituted a smaller National Unity Party (NUP) which was in fact, the former BSPP disguised in new clothes without any serving military members (Smith 1999: 20). It made many changes in the government's institutional framework and presented an image of taut, authoritarian administration, bent on change. Also following the coup, the army dropped the original ethnic names of its military units. This was the last step in erasing its original federal structure (Silverstein 2004). Restoration of law and order, preserving peace and tranquillity, facilitating smooth transportation and communications, and providing decent livelihood for the public were the professed objective of the junta. It promised to hold 'multi-party democratic elections', once these objectives had been accomplished (SLORC Declaration No. 1/88).

Although the Burmese coup of 1988 replaced the previous leadership with a new group of officers, it was not intended to shift power even among the military or between military factions. Rather it was designed to continue military rule by other means. It took place with the acquiescence of the authorities. In this phase of regime change, the ruling military junta has been managing a dual transition towards "multi-party electoral democracy", and a market-oriented economic system (Than 2007: 340). Since its inception, junta's legitimacy and authority has been contested by the legally constituted political opposition and a number of Western states and non-governmental organisations.

After the upheaval of 1988, multi-party election was a contingent choice to prevent its recurrence and together with the economic openness constitute the military's development paradigm for the 1990s and beyond. Saw Maung in an address on January 9, 1990 vowed that the army would stand by the election result and hand over to the elected government (Smith 1999: 23). A large number of political parties emerged at the close of registration numbering 235. Out of these, 93 ended up fielding candidates. Altogether there were 2209 candidates representing 93 parties and 87 independents. Although 492 single-seat constituencies were established, only 485 were contested in the elections held on 27 May 1990. Out of the elections which followed 479 seats were won by 27 parties and independents won 6 seats. The NLD won 392 seats and claimed victory (Table 3.1).

Table 3.1: Multi-party General Election in 1990

General Statistics of Elections		
Constituencies	:	492
Number in which election held	:	485
Eligible voters (485 constituencies)	:	20,818,313
Vote cast (72.6%)	:	15,112,524
Valid votes cast (60.3%)	:	13,253,606
Candidates	:	2,296 (2,209 from Parties, 87 independents)
Elected		485 (479 from Parties, 6 independents)
NLD seats	:	392
NUP seats	:	10
SNLD	:	23
Other parties	:	74
Independants	:	06

Source: Democratic Voice of Burma Documentation "The 1990 Multi-Party Democracy General Election". http://www.ibiblio.org/obl/docs4/1990_multi-party_elections.pdf

Elections, which in 1990 gave an overwhelming majority to the pro-democracy National League for Democracy (NLD), have simply been ignored. A stand-off between the military and the NLD ensued. The party, demanding the army convened a meeting of the *Pyithu Hluttaw* (Peoples Assembly) to form a new government under its auspices, was confronted by the army which persisted in stating that until a new Constitution was promulagated, the SLORC would continue to hold all legislative, executive and judicial power (Taylor 2005: 23). As, such, the 1990 elections did not lead to the formation of a government and the implementation of the election results has been a bone of contention between the junta and its political detractors (Than 2007: 342). Having made a massive miscalculation, the SLORC simply refused to hand over power, claiming in July 1990 that the election had only been for a constitutional assembly, and that a new election would have to be held once a new constitution had been written (SLORC Declaration 1/90).

In the years following the 1990 election, Myanmar's Generals focused on four objectives (Fink 2001: 77). First, they sought to expand greatly the size of the armed forces in order to be in a stronger position against their armed and unarmed opponents. As a result, the number of soldiers was increased and new bases were constructed throughout the country.[2] Second, the ruling generals worked to break-up the organizational structure of the pro-democracy movement and particularly the NLD. Third, they attempted to neutralize the ethnic nationalities by making cease-fire agreement with almost all of the armed groups. And fourth, they tried to improve the economy by opening up the country to trade and foreign investment.

The nationalization of industries, twenty-six years of central economic planning, and the curtailment of almost all foreign direct investment, ensured the destruction of the Burmese economy (McCarthy 2000a: 234). Recognizing that the socialist economic policies had been disastrous, the regime attempted to revive the economy encouraging private business and foreign investment (Fink 2001: 77). According to Martin Smith (1977: 23), "if Ne Win's *Buurmese Way to Socialism* was not exactly buried, it was most certainly dead". The SLORC undertook reforms in the name of "open door market economy of Myanmar" and has been using this "open door economy" and other measures since 1988 to improve its international image and attract foreign direct investment (Maung 1997: 503). It promulgated a liberal foreign investment law in December 1988. This has been regarded as a major step towards liberalization and an attempt to redress the capital deficiency caused by the cessation of Official Development Assistance (ODA). A number of institutional, legal and administrative reform measures were introduced over the next fifteen years (Than 2007: 355). These included the revoking of restrictions in agricultural trade and the relaxing of restrictions on production, milling, storing, transport, marketing and pricing of major crops. To facilitate economic development, SLORC initiated infrastructure projects such as roads, bridges and irrigation canals throughout the country, although in many cases they were completed by forced labourers under duress. Fertilizers were imported and efforts were made to make the agricultural sector more productive (Fink 2001: 80). Other measures included—reformulation of corporate procedures; revision of regulations and procedures on domestic and foreign trade; reactivation and reconstitution of chambers of commerce and business associations; and transforming municipal authorities into development committees.

As a part of the cosmetic reform procedure, international renaming of the country as *Myanmar Naing Ngan* (Union of Myanmar) took place in June 1989. It was followed by Burmanisation of most public names and titles (Smith 1999: 21). This modernization and expansion was further enhanced by a restructuring of the military bureaucracy. It saw the creation of two new regional commands—Tenasserim Coastal and Kegtung, as well as three regional administrative commands—all in pivotal ethnic minority border areas where military presence had previously been week (Smith 1999: 426). Barring few of these attempts, restructuring of the civil bureaucracy, however, remained a low priority amid the prolonged struggle between the military government and the political opposition (pro-democratic NLD) and the military's attempt at state building and consolidation (Mutebi 2005: 152).

In conjunction with the reformation drive, the military has actively plunged into the new business world through a policy, it termed 'Productive Establishment' (Smith 1999: 426). The main vehicle for this transformation was a new military company—the Union of Myanmar Economic Holdings (UMEH), which had been set-up in 1990. Besides, UMEH, the military owned and operated a number of other conglomerates, the most significant being the Myanmar Economic Corporation. These became a major force in the private sector and are engaged in banking, construction, external trade, manufacturing and gems (Than 2007: 392).

In transition to a market-oriented economy, Myanmar experienced the inevitable economic distortions, uncertainties and instabilities (Mutebi 2005: 152). After some modest growth during the mid-1990s, Myanmar once again faced economic problems (Ng May 2008: 58). The country suffered from declining investments, a severe depletion of foreign reserve and rampant inflation (Fink 2001: 77). Although in the first few years foreign direct investment flows quickly became significant. Tourism, textiles, mining, gas and oil became major developmental sectors (McCarthy 2000a: 244-45). But in the wake of the Asian financial crisis in 1997, these flows mainly from regional powers were severely truncated. Although there has never been any realistic expansion in export-oriented industries under *Tatmadaw*, except for the illegal trade, Myanmar's economy was not directly influenced by the contagion affect of the Asian financial crisis. Nevertheless, the *Tatmadaw's* goal of acquiring foreign exchange reserves by legal means was seriously curtailed by the direct impact of the financial crisis upon its ASEAN neighbours and Japan (McCarthy 2000a: 254). This has been supplemented by the pressure from the West and the poor economic management by the regime (Taylor 2005: 24; Ng May 2008: 58; Smith 1999: 432). As a result of the Asian economic crisis, foreign investment approvals fell by more than 70 per cent in the financial year 1997-98. Furthermore, tourists visits fell below significantly from an estimated 1 million in 1996 to a sharp decline in 1997 and continued to decrease in 1998, largely due to the regional instability caused by the Asian depression (Guyot 1998: 93). The regime had no expertise in economic planning and the generals were unwilling to delegate responsibility to trained economists (Fink 2001: 77). Inflation was estimated to have run at the rate of 20-40 per cent per year. Corruption was rampant due to trade, rising prices and foreign exchange controls imposed by the SLORC. The economy remained primarily an inefficient command economy with a nation-wide black market (Maung 1997: 504).

At the same time, the military regimes were scoring victories in the long standing battles with armed groups (Fink 2001: 80). In 1989, the Communist Party of Burma (CPB) collapsed. The ethnic minority faction within the CPB broke off and agreed to ceasefire with the regime in return for the minimal *Tatmadaw* interference in their internal affairs. In early and mid-90s, the SLORC was successful in splitting the armed Democratic Alliance of Burma which included many of the ethnic nationalist armies who had previously agreed to negotiate with the regime only as an allaince. The Pao National Organization was the first to break with its allies and made a ceasefire deal with SLORC in March 1991.[3] Others including the powerful Kachin Independence Organization soon followed, leaving only a few diehard groups to battle on by themselves.[4] Most of the groups felt that they could not compete with the increasingly powerful *Tatmadaw*, and they would be better off signing a deal that would give them continued control over some territory as well as chance to bring development to the civilians in their areas.

In the meanwhile, the junta sought to institute a legitimate role for the military in public life by holding a National Convention to write a new Constitution (Smith 1999; Taylor 2005: 2006; Than 2007). The National Convention was launched on October 2, 1992. The junta first convened the convention in January 1993. By September 1993, a detailed set of 104 basic principles endorsed by the National Convention Convening Committee (NCCC) had been established as a basis for future deliberations. The Convention was aborted in 1996 after NLD delegates walked out in protest, saying it was undemocratic (Taylor 2005: 23). It then went on eight years of long recess after April 1996, the steering committee continued to sit frequently for deliberations (Than 2007: 343). In the intermittent sessions that dragged on through a decade represented SLORC political vision, in which military's dominant role would be formalized in an ostensibly multi-party system of civilian government (Smith 1999: 128). The topic of holding a reconstituted 'National Constitutional Convention' dominated Myanmar's politics for past several years. The advent of National Convention, however, was accompanied by a great deal of international attention as Asian and European governments sought ways in which to assist the process of political reconciliation in Myanmar (Taylor

2006: 6). The convention was resurrected in May 2004 without NLD representatives. It completed its task on September 3, 2007.

The regime continued to face challenges in the late 90s, as it struggled with a weakening economy and sustained opposition from domestic political groups and foreign organization and government. Foreign investment began declining in the mid-90s due to poor economic management and constantly changing regulations. The Asian economic crisis in 1997 and Daw Aung San Suu Kyi's repeated calls for foreign businesses to stay out also resulted in reduced investment. Throughout the late 90s, inflation was running in double digit numbers eroding the value of fixed salaries and leading hundreds of thousands of Burmese to seek work outside the country (Fink 2001: 94). In spite of the introduction of the market forces and opening of the economy to local and international private initiatives, the statist legacy and the interventionist role of the state has remained pivotal. The primacy of the state's role in relation to non-state institutions was taken for granted by the ruling elite and has made the attempts by the regime to institute a 'market economy' open to private initiatives extremely problematic in Myanmar (Than 2007: 394).

3.1.6 SPDC Regime: 1998-2008

As a result of the military government's second major shake-up since 1988, in November 1997, the SLORC was replaced by the new State Peace and Development Council (SPDC). Following this a 19 member committee was formed and a new Cabinet was also announced (Smith 1999: 433). The generals in the SLORC and the SPDC have relied on an expansion of military, the staffing of the administrative offices with loyal servicemen, and the creation of a new mass organisation to widen and deepen their control over the general population. The regime increased the *Tatmadaw's* presence in cities and towns throughout the country, building dozens of new military compounds. If mass protests were to break out again, there would be troops everywhere to take action. The number of military intelligence agents was also increased infiltrating opposition organisations and monitoring soldiers as well (Fink 2001: 94-95). The regime appointed a number of military men to ward, township and regional administrative positions, but it also tried to woo the masses through the establishment of Union Solidarity and Development Association (USDA). USDA was purportedly a social organization founded on September 15, 1993 (Bowman 2007: 8). But it was headed by Senior Genereal Than Shwe and was often used to defend the interests of the regime. The regime sought to turn the USDA into a counter force against the NLD and students activists working for the restoration of the democracy (Smith 1999: 429). The authorities also gave military training to some USDA youth and used them to initimidate and attack Daw Aung San Suu Kyi and her supporters. The aim was to make it appear that the people and not just the regime were opposed to her and the NLD (Fink 2001: 96). Periodically, the USDA organized mass rallies throughout the country to demonstrate support for military rule and to denounce the NLD. In parallel, the SPDC is trying to organise a political and administrative structure that can pursue its agenda during the latter stages of the roadmap, a structure headed by the USDA, which is being groomed to be the dominant political actor in a future multi-party state (Bowman 2007: 2).

Since its overwhelming victory in the 1990 elections, the NLD has progressively developed and refined its policy position. It was taken further in 1998. In September that year, the Committee Representing the Peoples' Parliament (CRPP)—the NLD's answer to the regime's consistent refusal to call the elected Parliament—created 10 smaller committees, each charged with certain policy studies (Sleth 2001: 7-8). On several occasions, the leaders of armed ethnic organisations wrote individual and joint statement declaring their support for Daw Aung San Suu Kyi and the democratic struggle. Despite NLD's efforts to develop closer relations with ethnic nationality leaders, the regime continued to drive wedges between them. The armed ethnic groups were often reluctant to do anything that might jeopardise their ceasefire agreements[5] (Fink 2001: 98-99). Thus, as long as the *Tatmadaw* was in control, most of the leaders of the armed ethnic organisation felt it necessary to cooperate with the regime.

Ethnic Pao minority in Myanmar has gained considerable economic freedom as result of its accommodation with Burmese junta, who control possibly most repressive state in world. Pao, by agreeing to ceasefire with generals who run country, have won themselves civil rights and economic opportunities all but unimaginable to most Burmese. In addition to Pao, at least 15 other armed ethnic minorities have ended decades of bloodshed and are doing business with the military. For Generals, agreements with minority groups has brought end to series of expensive insurgent wars and freed them to focus state resources on saving themselves with ever-expanding web of repression as key to their continued rule. Deals between Generals and ethnic minorities have weakened hand of country's primary opposition group, whose leader is Daw Aung San Suu Kyi (*New York Times* 2000).

Meanwhile, on November 7, 2005, at an auspicious hour selected by astrologers, Myanmar's ruling junta shifted the national capital from Yangon to Naypyidow located in Kyatpyae Village of Pyinmana Township of Mandalay Division. Naypyidaw means "Royal City", but is also translated as "abode of kings". Pyinmana in Mandalay Division was chosen as the new capital because "it is centrally located and has quick access to all parts of the country.[6] The location confers the new capital many advantages, which the military regime did not enjoy in Yangon. "There was a real concern that the soldiers were becoming contaminated by the masses in Yangon and being made soft by the increased standard of living in Yangon: the restaurants, the consumer goods," says Larry Jagan. "So this was a way, really, of isolating and insulating the military so they would remain loyal." This may be the world's only national capital without mobile phone service or international flight connections (*Indian Express* 2007). According to Soe Minn, "Myanmar's paranoid military feels safe in a denuded area nestled among mountain jungle, aloof from the demands for democracy that are popping up elsewhere in the country".[7] Although it had been known for some time that a new strategic command centre was being built near Pyinmana, the sudden announcement in November 2005 that the entire government would start moving soon after came as a shock to the world (Pederson 2007: 4). The move to Naypyidaw has meant that they are now more remote and alienated from the general community and, most importantly, less in contact with the local communities than is the *Sangha*. As a result of this, the shift to Naypyidaw may lead to a more fragile state than they had expected (McCarthy 2008). The civil servants and the military contingents have found themselves frustrated as the shifting has affected their social and family life adversely.

However, by 2007, the regime had not been able to raise the standard of living of the majority of the domestic population. While military Generals' families and their friends managed to amass fortunes through virtual monopolies over many of the most lucrative businesses, ordinary Burmese businessmen found that without the necessary bribes and connections, they were not able to participate in the new market economy. Water and electricity shortages became acute in 1998-99, with frequent blackouts in Rangoon, and some rural towns receiving electricity only once every three to five days. Businesses and home suffered alike. The government's decision on 15 August 2007 to cut fuel subsidies, causing a sudden surge in fuel prices, was the spark that ignited a nation waiting to explode (Kingston 2008: 6). The sudden increases in official prices were 66 per cent for gasoline, 100 per cent for diesel fuel, and 500 per cent for CNG.

Four days later, the '8888' Generation student leaders and pro-democracy activists staged a powerful demonstration against this fuel price hike and other mass protests followed throughout the week (McCarthy 2008: 298-314). The crackdown which followed after the peaceful protests over fuel prices is a setback for the country and has the effect of calling into question the government's commitment to democratization (Burma Net News 2007).[8] The protestors pointed out the economic mismanagement of the SPDC regime. Although the military regime claimed as a 'Government of Burma' after a brutal and bloody coup in 1988, it has not played the required roles in an economy as a government (Myo 2007).[9] The protests in 2007 were a consequence of Burma's dire economic circumstances and it was supposed to remain explosive unless the needs of the vast majority remained neglected (Kingston 2008: 8).

On 5 September, more than 2,000 Buddhist monks staged a protest march in the Myanmar city of Pakokku to fight for democracy in the country. It came a day after soldiers fired teargas and warning shots to disperse a similar demonstration against Myanmar's ruling generals. They were marching very peacefully, just chanting prayers and holy scriptures. "No slogans, no demands" (ITN 2007). The increasing involvement of monks, who were key players in a 1988 mass uprising, is a sign that the dissent that broke out in August, over the rise in fuel prices, is intensifying. However, the demonstrators were attacked and beaten by members of the security forces, and possibly the USDA. This mistreatment of the country's highly revered Buddhist 'clergy' (or *Sangha*) so outraged some young monks that they immediately began organising their own country-wide protest movement (Sleth 2008: 281-97). News of the beating of monks at Pakokku rapidly spread through monasteries across the country, after which a newly formed group called the All Burma Monks Alliance (ABMA) issued a leaflet giving the SPDC to meet its demands or face a religious boycott by the deadline of 17 September. These demands constituted—apologise to the monks for the Pakokku violence; immediately reduce commodity prices including fuel, rice, and cooking oil prices; release all political prisoners including Aung San Suu Kyi and those arrested during the current protests; and an immediate dialogue with the "democratic forces" to resolve the suffering of the people (HRW 2008: 13). The SPDC ignored these demands (McCarthy 2008: 298-314). Not only did they seek economic reforms to alleviate the suffering of the lay population, on whom they depended, but they also demanded an official apology for the gross disrespect shown to the *Sangha*. The generals have favoured using civilian gangs and members of its feared USDA social network to break up protests.

Myanmar made international headlines, when the military junta ordered a crackdown on protestors marching through Yangon calling for an end to their 45-year rule. A Japanese photographer was shot in front of the Sule Pagoda. Monks were beaten and killed. On 26 September, armed soldiers and police opened fire on a large demonstration in Rangoon. That night, out of the public eye, a number of the city's Buddhist monasteries were raided, and hundreds of monks were forcibly detained. The following day, and for the rest of that week, any protesters who dared to march were met with tear gas, baton charges and, on several occasions, lethal force (Sleth 2008: 281-97).

Myanmar's only Internet server was shut and text and picture messaging on mobiles, stopped. To quote Soe Myint, "Radio is the only means available to the leaders who are in hiding. They broadcast their instructions to the four radio stations that are operating outside Myanmar. At present, all the people of Myanmar are listening to the radio. The military cannot jam the radios as they are on shortwave and if they do so they will affect their own wireless systems. It's an uprising driven by people from all walks of life—except for the police and the military. It's a revolution of the people and has spread to 50 cities since August 15".[10] According to Ashin Panna Siri, "The images of thousands of red robed monks, bare footed and bold quietly standing up to the armed might of riot policemen and tanks were indelible. Somehow their silence seems to be loud and brutal".[11]

These visible protests by the Buddhist clergy, beamed across the entire world have stripped the Burmese generals of the last layer of legitimacy. By overturning their alms bowls and refusing to accept donations from the military, the participating monks threatened to expose the veil of political legitimacy that the current rulers have attempted to maintain internally since the early 1990s (McCarthy 2008: 298-314). It is clear from the continuing street protests that this time the seeds of dissent may have been sown much deeper than the military estimates. The SPDC has shamed the military as an institution in the eyes of the people and, more importantly, damaged relations with the *Sangha*, the repository of moral authority in Myanmar (Kingston 2008: 17). Bertil Lintner predicts that the Saffron Revolution is "the beginning of the end of military rule in Myanmar. It may take time but it clearly will end. The moment an officer stands up and says enough is enough it will all crumble" (quoted in Kingston 2008: 18).

The military regime managed to severely damage the organisational capacity of the pro-democracy movement, but it was not able to a build a prosperous nation. The 'saffron revolution' brought to light, the fact that the generals have lost an enormous amount of legitimacy by committing violence against the very institution they are meant to support and whose traditions they promote, the *Sangha* (McCarthy 2008). The new constitution which took 16 long years to complete has replaced the SPDC regime based on the military engineered Seven-point Roadmap to Democracy in Myanmar in 2003.[12] The result of Constitutional Referendum held in May 2008 in which 92 per cent of the voters showed their willingness to adopt the new Constitution and subsequently the November 2010 elections have opened a new agenda for reforms and change in the country.

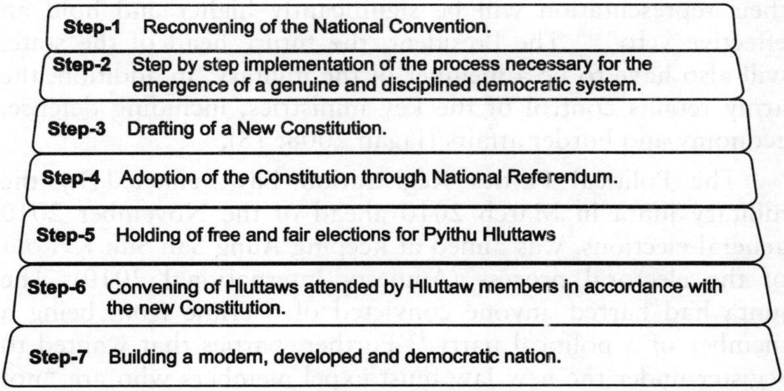

Fig. 3.1: Seven-point Roadmap to Military Way of Democracy.

3.1.7 Democratic Transition and Reconciliation in Myanmar 2008 Onwards

The new Constitution approved by the overwhelming majority of the population (superficially) in May 2008 referendum not only enshrines the junta's hold on power, but effectively excludes Suu Kyi from office. According to Constitutional Principle approved by the National Convention, the President should be an indigeneous Burmese. The Constitution lays down that "the President shall be a person who has stayed in the state continuously for a minimum of 20 years at the time of the election of the State President. Further, either of his parents, spouse, any legitimate child shall not be a loyal subject to any foreign government or a person under the influence of a foreign government or citizen of an alien country". This has disempowered NLD leader Aung San Suu Kyi from contesting Presidential election as her husband was a British national.[13] Under the Charter, a quarter of seats in both houses of new Parliament would be guaranteed for the military—at the National as well as regional and State Assemblies. The draft Constitution makes it virtually impossible to amend the clauses because more than three quarters of the members of both the houses of the Parliament need to approve any amendment. According to Soe Min, "given that the military holds at least one quarter of the seats, their representation will be significantly higher and hold an effective veto".[14] The President, the future head of the state, will also have to be a member of the military. In addition, the army retains control of the key ministries, including defense, economy and border affairs (Jagan 2008: 18).

The Political Parties Registration Law, enacted by the military junta in March 2010 ahead of the November 2010 general elections, was aimed at keeping Aung San Suu Kyi out of the electoral process (Amnesty International 2010). The junta had barred anyone convicted of a crime from being a member of a political party.[15] Further, parties that wanted to register under the new law must expel members who are "not in conformity with the qualification to be members of a party." This meant that Suu Kyi could not contest the elections, and the National League for Democracy (NLD) would expel her if it wanted to be eligible to participate in the election process. The junta also offered a carrot to the NLD by removing the seals on the regional offices of the party. They wanted the NLD to contest the election in order to give the polls some credibility. Henceforth, 300 NLD offices were allowed to reopen. But the junta also wanted a very weak NLD, with Suu Kyi completely out of the picture. This posed a dilemma before NLD whether to participate by expelling Suu Kyi or to completely boycott the elections. The party was, however, disbanded for failing to register under the new election law.

The 2010 elections installed a nominally civilian government which in practice is mostly a 'constitutionalised' façade for ongoing military rule (Turnell 2011: 148). The election was rigged giving military's USDP around 60 per cent of the contested seats, over and above 25 per cent of the seats reserved for the military (Economist 2011a). The President, Vice President, head of the USDP all are former generals. The results of the elections are presented in Table 3.2.

An analysis of the election result shows that the military-dominated Parliament has emerged out of the recent General elections held after a gap of twenty years. The junta's political vehicle, the Union Solidarity and USDP, had a landslide victory with 76 per cent of the total votes. Twenty-three out of 37 approved parties successfully contested the elections. The USDP won 129 out of 168 seats in the House of Nationalities, 259 out of 325 seats in the People's Assembly, and 494 out of 661 seats in Regional and State Parliaments. It had 79 per cent of lower house seats, 77 per cent of the seats in Upper House and a 75 per cent stake in the seven state and seven regional assemblies. The National Unity Party (NUP) which is supposed to have close links with the military stood at the second position like in the previous election of 1990 with a total of 64 seats. The poll was marred by allegations of fraud and intimidation. The main opposition party, a splinter group of the erstwhile NLD—National Democratic Force (NDF) got twelve seats in both the houses and in total just 16 seats. The three major ethnic parties were, however, able to make their position in the top five slots. They are the Shan Nationalities Democratic Party (SNDP), with 58 seats; the Rakhine Nationalities Development Party (RNDP) with 35 seats, and All Mon Region Democracy Party (AMRDP) with 16 seats.

In addition, 25 per cent of the seats in all legislative chambers are reserved for serving soldiers. A total of 166 mid-ranking officers were notified about their appointment as parliamentarians. The military and the USDP, which is mostly constituted by the retired soldiers or junta cronies, jointly control 84 per cent of the National Parliament. Rest of the parties such as the NUP, SNDP, RNDP, AMRDP, NDF and others constitute just 16 per cent of the seats in the legislature. The biggest pro-democracy party, the National Democratic Force, has less than 2 per cent, with just 12 seats.

Table 3.2: Results of 2010 Election

PARTIES	House of Nationalities (Amyotha Hluttaw) A		House of Representatives (Pyithu Hluttaw) B		Total Seats in both the Houses C (A + B)	Regional Parliament D		Total (C + D)	
USDP	129 (76.7%)		259 (79.6%)		388 (78.7%)	494 (74.8%)		882 (76.4%)	
NUP	05		12			47		64	
SNDP	03		18			37		58	
RNDP	07		09			19		35	
NDF	04	39	08	66	105	04	167	16	272
AMRDP	04		03			09		16	
Others	16		16			51		83	
Total Elected	168		325		493	661		1154	
Appointed (military 25%)	56		110		166	222		388	
Grand Total	224		435		659	883		1542	

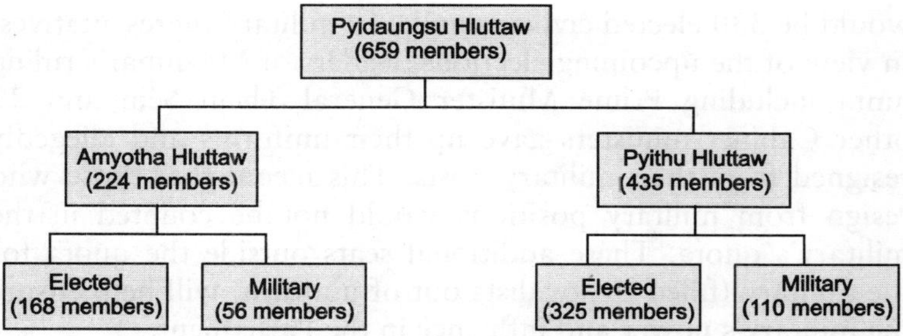

Fig. 3.2: Composition of Pyidaungsu Hluttaw.

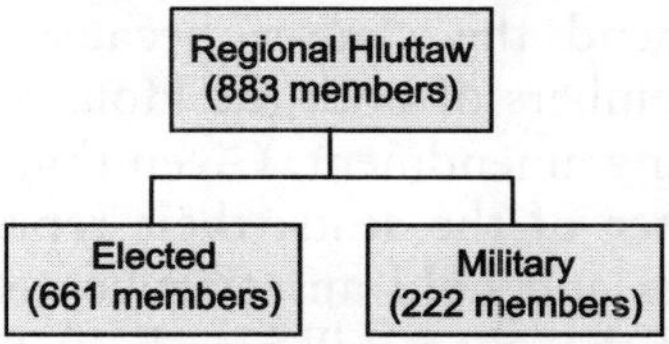

Fig. 3.3: Composition of Regional Hluttaw.

The release of the Nobel laureate Aung San Suu Kyi after seven years of house arrest in November 2010 just three days after the Elections has been a welcome step for the pro-democracy movement in Myanmar. But the fact that the restrictions over her movement is likely to continue for some time demonstrates that the authorities have just released her as a symbolic gesture. The release has, however, come at a time when the entire Western world is opposed to the way elections have been conducted and the new Constitution imposed upon the people of Myanmar. The leadership is, in fact, on a goodwill mission and wants to show to the world that they are genuinely moving towards democracy and probably, this is the time when they can easily engage with the rest of the world under the garb of democratisation. At this stage, they really don't anticipate any threat from the 'Lady' as the Burmese Nobel laureate is popularly called, since her political party has been officially disbanded and the new Constitution restricts her from contesting any future elections in Myanmar.

Under the Charter, a quarter of seats in both Houses of new Parliament would be guaranteed for the military—at the National as well as regional and State Assemblies, i.e. in a newly created 440-member House of Representatives there would be 330 elected civilians and 110 military representatives. In view of the upcoming elections, leaders of Myanmar's ruling junta including Prime Minister General Thein Sein and 22 other Cabinet ministers gave up their uniforms and allegedly resigned from their military posts. This meant that those who resign from military positions would not be counted in the military's quota. These additional seats outside the quota for the military (filled by loyalists out of uniform) will help ensure the military's power and influence in the Parliament.

The draft Constitution further makes it virtually impossible to amend the clauses because more than three quarters of the members of both the Houses of the Parliament need to approve any amendment. Given that the military holds at least one quarter of the seats, their representation will be significantly higher and hold an effective veto. The President, the future head of the state, will also have to be a member of the military. In addition, the army retains control of the key ministries, including defense, economy and border affairs.

Nonetheless, military regime has achieved a multi-party elected parliament for first time in 50 years. According to Trevor Wilson (2010), "it also achieved quasi—'civilianisation' of government, albeit run by the same people without their uniforms. The elections have also created a new level of political power to reflect quasi-federal nature of the Burmese nation, but the prospects for effective functioning of the new regional assemblies is not clear".

In Myanmar, the elections held after a gap of twenty years in 2010 has paved the way for a transition from military rule to a supposedly civilian administration and democratic opening. But the fact that the polls were swept by the pro junta political party—Union Solidarity and Development Party (USDP) and its allies exposes the myth of democratisation in the country. In the absence of any clear opposition with National League of Democracy being disbanded, the election has widely been seen as an attempt to legitimize military rule behind a mask of civilian government. Civilian dictatorship sought to be established in the post election Myanmar characterise an illusion of multi-party democracy at the local and the national level while effectively stripping the legality and efficacy of a free and fair election. The regime alleges that it is preparing for a transition period from military rule to a supposedly civilian administration popularly conceived by the leadership as *Disciplined Democracy*.

Notes

1. Interview with Zaw Win Aung, Chief of Bureau, Democratic Voice of Burma and Federation of Trade Union, Burma on October 25, 2008.
2. For instance, the number of soldiers increased from 1,80,000 in 1988 to over 4,00,000 by 1999 (Fink 2001: 77).
3. The Pao people are one of the ethnic minority groups in Shan State. The Christian population among Pao people is less than 1% as they are deeply rooted in Buddhism. The Pao National Organization (PNO) has 300 regular fighters (90% Pao, 10% Shan, Kayah, Palaung and others). The Pao number approximately 1.6 million.
4. The Kachin Independence Organization (KIO) counts more than five thousand regular soldiers. The Kachin people number some two million persons, who live in northernmost Myanmar.
5. While the ceasefires had not resulted in the granting of ethnic rights and political autonomy, they did mean the end of decades long civil war and far less suffering for the civilian population.
6. Pyinmana is located approximately 400 km from Yangon, in the Southern salient of the Mandalay Division. It is a key communication hub with roads and rail leading to the Northeast, Southwest, and Southeast. It also provides easy access to the Shan, Kayah and Karen states, which have been the scene of powerful minority insurgencies for over five decades. Its historic association dates back to the days of Myanmar's struggle for independence led by Gen. Aung San. It served as the military headquarters of his resistance army. Infrastructure including roads and buildings to house the new capital has been under development for the last four years.
7. Based on interview with Soe Myint, Radio and T.V. Reporter, Democratic Voice of Burma.
8. Accorging to the United Nations envoy Ibrahim Gambari, "These incidents of recent times cannot be seen in any other way than a setback for Myanmar". He further stated that, "They are all the more disappointing as they not only have the effect of calling into question the stated commitment to democratization and national reconciliation by the authorities, but also make it more difficult to maintain support, international support, for engagement with Myanmar at a time when we believe strongly that the country needs international assistance in addressing the many pressing challenges, from political and human rights

issues to humanitarian and socio-economic problems." (Burma Net News 2007).

9. Government's first role in an economy is to achieve macroeconomic and political stability. Government's second role in an economy is to improve general microeconomic capacity of the economy. Government's third role is to establish the overall macroeconomic rules and incentives governing competition that will encourage productivity growth. For details see Myo 2007.
10. Based on an interview with Soe Myint, at School of International Studies, JNU on October 30, 2007. He is the managing editor of the Delhi-based news agency *Mizzima News*.
11. Based on interview with Ashin Panna Siri, a Buddhist monk who participated in the demonstration.
12. The seven steps of the political reforms are:
    (1) Reconvening of the National Convention that has been adjourned since 1996.
    (2) After the successful holding of the National Convention, step by step implementation of the process necessary for the emergence of a genuine and disciplined democratic system.
    (3) Drafting of a new constitution in accordance with basic principles and detailed basic principles laid down by the National Convention.
    (4) Adoption of the constitution through national referendum.
    (5) Holding of free and fair elections for Pyithu Hluttaws (Legislative bodies) according to the new Constitution.
    (6) Convening of Hluttaws attended by Hluttaw members in accordance with the new Constitution.
    (7) Building a modern, developed and democratic nation by the state leaders elected by the Hluttaw; and the government and other central organs formed by the Hluttaw.
13. Based on Presentation by Dr. Tint Swe, "Burmese Military's Constitution: Perpetual Military Authoritarianism".
14. Based on the interview with Soe Myint.
15. Pyithu Hluttaw Election Law, SPDC Law No. 3/2010.

Chapter 4

Political Transition in Myanmar

After nearly five decades of military rule, elections in November 2010 and a new Constitution in 2008 were apparently meant to usher in a return to civilian rule. The victory of NLD in the recent by-elections has, particularly, been an attempt by the reform-minded ex-generals in Parliament, to make use of Daw Suu Kyi to boost its credibility. The regime needs Suu Kyi in Parliament to bolster the authority of its own political system and spur on easing Western sanctions. NLD is the largest opposition party in the national legislature with 43 seats and 6.4 per cent of the overall seats in the Parliament's Lower and Upper Houses. Several ethnic and minority parties are also waiting to embrace the NLD in the legislature as its presence will boost overall confidence in the opposition. The reform process, however, in Myanmar is scared by the reformists and hardliners in the army. The hardliners have become more concerned after the last by-elections when military backed USDP could just get one out of the 45 seats. Nevertheless, resolving the ethnic issue will be Myanmar's biggest challenge now. Overcoming of sixty year old ethnic conflict will not be easy and the government will have to do a great deal to build the trust necessary to move beyond temporary ceasefires to resolve the underlying political issues.

4.1 PROCESS OF TRANSITION

The process of transition to democracy can be described with the help of the following overlapping phases (Shin 1994:

43; Sorenson 1998: 39-40; Gill 2000: 43; Carothers 2002: 7; Huntington 1991: 35, 114; Diamond 2000: 414; Linz and Stepan 1998: 48):

(i) the preparatory phase, or decay of authoritarian rule characterised by a political struggle leading to the breakdown of the non-democratic regime;

(ii) the transition phase, where clear-cut elements of a democratic order are established;

(iii) the consolidation phase, where the new democracy is further developed, and eventually, democratic practices become an established part of the political culture; and

(iv) the maturity phase, where the maturing of a stable political order takes place. This phase also looks at the institutionalization of democratic practices within state institutions.

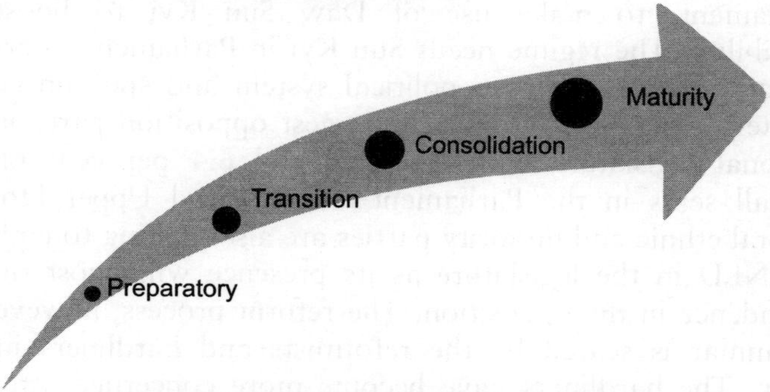

Fig. 4.1: Process of Democratic Transition.

The phases, however, do not represent a pre-determined path that all countries will or must follow. There is no historical law which says that regimes must move from authoritarianism to democratic system. However, it must be realized here that the phases outlined are not necessarily negotiated in a smooth or linear manner. There may be crisis or setbacks (Sorenson 1998: 39). The options are all cast in terms of the speed and direction with which countries move on the path (Carothers 2002: 7). The result of the regime change need not necessarily be democracy. It could also lead to replacement of one authoritarian regime by another (Gill 2000: 43). A more accurate description of typical pattern in the developing world is an uneasy fluctuation between authoritarianism and frail democracy. A large majority of the current transition are in the early phases of moving toward democracy. More specifically, they can be described as restricted democracies that are feeble and unconsolidated and plagued by acute social and economic problems.

Following the four stages of democratisation mentioned in the literatures on democratic transition which has forward and backward linkages between each successive stage, Myanmar may now be categorised to have surpassed Stage II (particularly after the 2010 elections). Although change has occurred in Myanmar and it is embarking on a new era of democratic reforms on the path of 'disciplined democracy', yet very few are optimistic about what it might bring in the long run. After the elections held on November 7, 2010 and release of Aung San Suu Kyi on November 13, 2010 there is a ray of hope for democracy and change in Myanmar. On 31 January 2011 a new Parliament was convened and on 30 March 2011, the erstwhile junta was dissolved handing over power formally to the new successor civilian government. Myanmar's former Prime Minister Thein Sein was sworn in as the country's new President, marking the end of the military body that has governed the Asian nation for decades. Tin Myint Oo and Sai Muak Kham would serve as Vice-Presidents. The President named 30 ministers and 39 deputy ministers to his government.

The effort is made by the newly convened Parliament and leadership to establish a façade of constitutional democracy. The new regime through various articles and speeches is trying to convince its citizens about move that cements the military's control of a new political system. Given below is an extract from an article published in the National Daily, *New Light of Myanmar*.

> The State is like a large boat. It must have a government like the captain, the administrative machinery like the

> boatmen, party organizations like the navigator, people like the passengers, economic forces like the rudder and the sails and economic infrastructures like the hull. Only with these characteristics plus concerted efforts, can the boat reach its destination smoothly. According to a political term, working harmoniously with the characteristics of a nation means being politically united.... In Myanmar, 98.12 percent of all eligible voters cast their ballots, and there has been a constitution approved by 92.48 percent of all the voters. There have been people's representatives elected through the elections held systematically in accord with the constitution. The Hluttaws at various levels formed with those representatives and a government will emerge soon, and Myanmar will reach the new democratic era. (*NLM* Dec. 8, 2010)

As a part of the attempt by the military regime to establish 'disciplined democracy' in Myanmar, SPDC announced the 'Seven-step Roadmap' in 2002 and as per this roadmap a new Constitution was drafted by the National Convention. In spite of the devastating cyclone Nargis in 2008, the SPDC proceeded with a referendum on a new Constitution in May 2008, which it claimed was approved by overwhelming majority of votes. The elections in 2010 were also the culmination of the junta's seven-step roadmap towards disciplined democracy. Less than a week after the elections, Myanmar's democracy icon and Nobel Peace Prize laureate, Aung San Suu Kyi, was released from house arrest. Now, she has won a place in the lower House of the Parliament when the NLD won 43 of 45 available seats in a historic April 1, 2012 by-election, thrashing President Thein Sein's ruling Union Solidarity and Development Party (USDP), the dominant force in the legislature.

The new national and regional parliaments are the centerpiece of the country's claimed return to civilian rule. Still, the new Constitution greatly inhibits the creation of a genuine civilian government in Myanmar. One reason is the reservation of 25 per cent of all seats in the national Parliament for military personnel (Turnell 2011: 139). It also assigns key ministerial portfolios such as Defense and Home Affairs exclusively to military representatives. Likewise, the Constitution grants extraordinary powers to an unelected "Commander in Chief of the Defense Services," who during a self-declared state of emergency may assume all legislative, executive, and judicial authority. Finally, constitutional amendments require the approval of over 75 per cent of parliamentary members, effectively giving the military a veto over constitutional change.

Although the change is coming slowly to the isolated country, yet it has a long way to go. Despite the obvious limitations of the parliamentary process, the members are hopeful that the government would sometime listen. It would prepare a ground for the next general elections in 2015. Most of the opposition parties, though they were against military engineered elections, yet they participated in it, thinking that it is only through engagement and reconciliation with the junta that they would be able to move towards greater freedom and openness and democratic reforms.

4.2 REFORM AGENDA OF THE NEW REGIME

We see a new political system emerging in Myanmar. Only the regime change in not enough, it has to be supplemented with the social and economic change. The newly elected civilian regime has emphasized on the fundamental rights of the citizens and the need for a clean and corruption free society. The President in his inaugural speech used the words like 'good governance' and 'democratic reforms'.

To quote the President Thein Sein,

> In transition to democracy, it is obligatory to promote democratic practices not only among the Hluttaw representatives but also among the people. To do so, I promise that our government will cooperate with the political parties in the hluttaws, good-hearted political forces outside the hluttaws and all social organizations.....

> Democracy will promote only hand in hand with good governance. This is why our government responsible for Myanmar's democracy transition will try hard to shape good administrative machinery....
>
> To safeguard the fundamental rights of citizens in line with the provisions of the constitution in the new democratic nation is high on our government's list of priorities. We guarantee that all citizens will enjoy equal rights in terms of law, and we will reinforce the judicial pillar....
>
> We will fight corruption in cooperation with the people as it harms the image of not only the offenders but also the nation and the people.... (*New Light of Myanmar*, 30 March 2011)

The new regime is also trying to convince the international community of the political changes and reforms that are taking place in the country. The leadership has endeavoured to end its international isolation by promoting the democratic icon Nobel Laureate Aung San Suu Kyi and allowing her party NLD to participate in the by-elections in April 2012 and rejoin mainstream politics.[1] ASEAN's decision to allow Myanmar to take up the Chairmanship of the body in 2014 has given the new regime acceptability in the region. Myanmar's leadership which has long counted on China as its main supporter has rolled out a series of reformist measure in the field of health, social security, education and mass media. This has been widely seen as part of its effort to gain domestic and international legitimacy. Furthermore, the new rapprochement marked by the US Secretary of State, Hillary Clinton's landmark visit to the country after more than fifty years of estrangement demonstrates that the process of reforms have gained momentum and recognition.[2]

These have given the new regime a degree of international acceptance, reduction of sanctions and the possibility of aid from international financial institutions. These cosmetic changes have helped to shift image perceptions, seen in the EU's dropping of some of its punitive measures in March 2011 and its coincident praise for the regime's "greater civilian character". United Nations official Vijay Nambiar followed this, saying the regime has demonstrated "very encouraging" signs after his visit in May 2011. The same has been reiterated by United Nations Human Rights Envoy to Myanmar Tomas Ojea Quintana who has described it as the 'key moment in Myanmar's history'. Most analysts believe the openness being shown by Myanmar's leaders is aimed in part at improving their image abroad with a view to ending decades of Western sanctions and consolidating power at home.

Although failure of regime performance in the economic front had delayed democracy in Myanmar, yet the new regime has taken all the possible steps for rebuilding the economy. President Thein Sein in his inaugural speech in the Parliament has focused on the 'economic might' for growth and development of the country. He has focused on agricultural development as well as industrialization to transform country into a developed, rich one with a lot of employment opportunities and high per capita income. The new regime invited a delegation from the International Monetary Fund (IMF) to visit in October 2011 to advise policymakers on how to tackle problems with the kyat currency, which has appreciated 20 per cent in a year, hurting farmers and exporters and bankrupting businesses. After months of inaction and simmering anger, the government in July 2011 cut taxes for exporters and has promised agriculture loans and price guarantees for millions of farmers, suggesting it may be concerned that any mishandling of bread and butter issues could see a repeat of bloody uprisings in 1988 and 2007 that were sparked by soaring inflation and fuel prices.

New laws are expected to come out in the subsequent sessions of the Parliament such as a labour law and social security law. The MPs have agreed to discuss promulgation of new comprehensive Social Security Insurance Law which is more comprehensive in its coverage than the 1954 Social Security Act.[3] This is in accordance with the articles 24, 26(b), 28(a), 31, 32(a) of the new Constitution. President Thein Sein has also mentioned that "In particular, we will create employment opportunities, stabilize commodity prices and encourage welfare and social security for the convenience of workers and labourers. And we will ensure that minimum pay scale meets current living costs. We guarantee that national workers inside and outside the nation enjoy all rights".

Health care has also been a major area of concern for the new government. In order to implement better health care facilities, government is committed towards improving the existing health care facilities—both in urban and rural areas at the same time it is also disseminating knowledge about seasonal and other fatal diseases such as AIDS, tuberculosis and malaria. President has focused on this issue in his inaugural speech and the MPs have also raised their concern in the Parliament about public health care, disease prevention and prevention and control of the epidemic.[4]

Myanmar is taking initiative to carry out education reform soon after the new government took office. President Thein Sein vowed to promote the national education up to international standard and work for the development of human resources in all seriousness.[5] The Vice-President Sai Mauk Kham has also called for mending the country's education system in order to meet the international level. Myanmar has been implementing a 30-year national education promotion plan since 2001-02 academic year, guaranteeing that every school-age child can receive good access to education and every citizen complete basic education under a plan being implemented with the cooperation of regional authorities, social organizations and parents of the students. It is also gearing up for the launch of compulsory primary education plan in 2011-12 academic year. Meanwhile, Myanmar authorities have started to draft law related to private school education as part of its move to open up education sector to private run and strengthen administration.

The 'environmental issues' is moving into a more high profile position in Myanmar these days, with political parties making it a priority in the new Parliament and more civic groups taking up the cause. The new government is drafting a new law for environmental conservation for proportionate development of the economic, social and environmental development. One of the latest signs of environmental activism is the formation of an environmental protection subcommittee by the National League for Democracy. Formed on April 27, 2011, the committee's mission is to represent environmental interests in the area of dam construction, irrigation projects and the agricultural use of chemical fertilizers and pesticides. In his inaugural address to Parliament, President Thein Sein talked about conservation of the environment at length, saying that he would weigh the need for economic development and the conservation of environment.[6] Vice-President Dr. Sai Mauk Kham has also stressed the need for environment conservation in terms of trees and forest so as to hand down the existing good condition of natural environment of the country to new generations. The government has also bowed to environmentalist and social activists by cancelling two high profile state projects: the Myitsone Dam hydropower project, and a coal-fired power plant in the Dawei deep-sea port project and industrial zone.

Human rights which had been given low priority for decades have also been advanced. It has set up a National Human Rights Commission which will safeguard the rights of its citizens. The panel would comprise 15 retired bureaucrats and academics. The latest human rights committee was formed on the advice of the United Nations Human Rights Envoy to Myanmar Tomas Ojea Quintana. The move follows steps by the newly-installed civilian administration to improve Myanmar's international reputation as well as relations with the country's Democracy movement. Although the issue of the release of more than 2,000 political prisoners and the concern about the ethnic conflict zones remains unresolved, yet the process to review and possibly amend or revoke arbitrary national legislation is underway. Tomás Ojea Quintana concluded at the end of his five-day mission to the South-East Asian nation, "This is a key moment in Myanmar's history and there are real opportunities for positive and meaningful developments to improve the human rights situation and bring about a genuine transition to democracy".

Myanmar's once watertight censorship board has in recent months undertaken reforms. The amendment to the country's press laws in March to allow the majority of non-news journals to bypass pre-censorship was accompanied by the announcement that two Thailand-based dailies, the *Bangkok Post* and *The Nation*, will soon be allowed to hit news-stands in Yangon. These events have helped to maneuvour the carefully crafted image of a government loosening its grip on the media as it moves steadily towards democratic reform. President Thein Sein mentioned in his inaugural speech that media is the fourth pillar of the nation and media laws needs to be amended in line with the provisions of the Constitution and that 'it is getting more and more developed'. The Information and Broadcasting Minister has also highlighted that there would be more freedom of press and the government has offered strong indications that it may relax media restrictions. Under the proposed changes, coverage on mostly benign subjects, including sports and entertainment, would no longer have to pass through the office of the censor before hitting news-stands.

In September 2011, pro-democracy icon Aung San Suu Kyi published her first article in the Burmese media for 23 years on the front page of *Pyithu Khit News Journal*, while *Messenger News* also ran an exclusive interview with the Nobel Laureate as its cover story. *Pyithu Khit* (People's Era) was permitted by the Burmese censorship board—the Press Scrutiny and Registration Division under the Ministry of Information—to publish Suu Kyi's article entitled "Holiday-1". It also carried a piece by one of her close aides—veteran journalist Win Tin's old article on Suu Kyi's father Aung San. For the last 23 years, even Suu Kyi's name or any symbols indirectly referring to her—such as "the lady," "the mother" or "the rose"—was banned in publications. This move is a part of the recent relaxation of control over media, seen as part of the new, nominally civilian government's effort to reach out to the democratic opposition in a bid to win greater international recognition. As Myanmar enters a new political phase, the international community should seize the opportunity to encourage greater openness and reforms.

The new regime has also tried to shed its pariah image by appointing U Myint as the economic adviser to the new President. He is supposed to be liberal minded and close to the democracy icon Aung San Suu Kyi. His appointment is being hailed by the newly appointed civilian regime. In a country whose economy is being controlled by cronies, U Myint faces a major challenge of rebuilding the economy amidst the dismal economic performance of the past five decades. It is believed that his appointment is suppose to send positive signals to the international community for liberalizing its attitude towards Myanmar and encourage investment opportunities in the country. The regime has also shown signs recently that it is seeking to improve its image by reaching out to the critics such as the opposition leader Aung San Suu Kyi who met the President Thein Sein in the sidelines of the Economic Development Forum organized in Naypyidaw on 20-21 August 2011.[7] She attended this workshop as a special guest. It is the latest olive branch from the army-backed regime that came to power after five decades of direct military rule. This move is based amid the call from the international community for the new regime to ensure Suu Kyi rights and freedom of movement.

Thein Sein's government has capitalized on the reform agenda through a carefully choreographed public relations campaign that began with last November's elections and the release of pro-democracy leader Aung San Suu Kyi and has continued with recent 'liberalisation reforms'. He has sought to dilute his hardline image with somewhat reformist rhetoric. Although there are skepticism about the parliamentary procedures and rules of conduct are yet not established properly, yet these sessions are likely to give us a better indication of the direction we can expect the country to take over the next four years. Many of the sessions are so curtailed that the critics call it a '15 minute Parliament'. Opposition members are not allowed to submit their questions and most of them seem to be disillusioned by its style and method.

Nevertheless, we find beginning of a parliamentary tradition for the people to voice their concern. It has at least opened up the space for different actors and parties to engage in the political process. Recently, the new regime has released about 200 political prisoners along with more than 6,000 other inmates in October 2011 as a part of its amnesty scheme. Furthermore, country's Independence Day on 4 January 2012 was marked by commuting sentences and apparently releasing more than 30 prisoners. This was followed by the announcement of the release of 651 political prisoners as a positive signal and an important step towards the full release of all political prisoners and a factor in the national reconciliation process (*Telegraph* 2012).

The civilian government of President Thein Sein has been working hard to show a new face to the world and to improve its relations with its critics at home and abroad. But there are many analysts who believe that the effort towards reform by the militarized government is just a 'survival attempt'. The regime has been accused for creating a façade for liberalization to prompt Western countries to lift sanctions imposed over the country's political and human rights record. It is a means of cementing their hold over the regime with a view towards long-term control. Opposition member, on the other hand, see the new government as merely a front for the military. It has raised hopes for change with a major 'charm' offensive.

4.3 CHALLENGES OF POLITICAL TRANSITION IN MYANMAR

After five decades of authoritarian rule in Myanmar, the country faces a plethora of challenges both in the domestic and external affairs. On the one hand, the need for building up democratic institutions and re-invigorating faith in Parliamentary procedures, multi-party democracy, reforms in the armed forces and national reconciliation demands attention. On the other hand, the international isolation of this 'hermit kingdom' needs to open itself to the outside world and move forward on the path of economic growth and development. Some of these major challenges have been looked upon in the following section.

4.3.1 Hardliners and Reformists

The reform process in Myanmar is scared by the reformists and hardliners in the army. Carothers (2002), in *The End of Transition Paradigm,* observes that democratization primarily occurs due to the opening, a period of democratic ferment and political liberalization in which cracks appear in the ruling dictatorial regime, with the most prominent fault line being that between hardliners and softliners.

According to Harn Yawnghwe, director of Brussels-based Euro-Burma Office (EBO), the country's top leadership is made up of two factions, divided by conflicting personal feelings and ways of thinking. He believes that the 'Gang of Four', i.e. the Vice-President #1 Tin Aung Myint Oo; the Upper House Speaker Khin Aung Myint; the Information Minister Kyaw Hsan; and the Finance Minister Hla Tun constitute the military-minded hard core supporters of the previous regime. "They have reportedly urged the Senior General (Than Shwe) to stage a comeback, but unless Thein Sein makes a big blunder thereby giving him sufficient excuse, it is unlikely he will return". On the other hand, the "Reformists", i.e. the President Thein Sein; the Lower House Speaker Thura Shwe Mann; the Railway Transport Minister Aung Min; and the Industry #1 Minister Soe Thein are all bent towards introducing Parliamentary practices and reforms for the new regime. However, the fence sitters are still the majority in the top echelon. "They are naturally waiting to see which direction the wind is blowing before they make up their minds", reaffirms Harn Yawnghwe.[8] The battle between reformers and hardliners has been gaining momentum with the liberals led by President Thein Sein and Speaker of Parliament Thura Shwe Mann. The hardliners have become more concerned after the last by-elections when military-backed USDP could just get one out of the 45 seats. These party members are coalescing into the main anti-reformist noise. This outcome is causing "disarray" within the ranks of the former ruling military and raising speculation about a backlash by hardliners.

The reformist-minded President Their Sein has quoted recently that "conservatives who do not have a reformist mindset will be left behind" while the country is on its path to change. Even the Vice-President Sai Mauk Kham also emphasised that "not only political, economic, administrative and social reforms are needed but there also needs to be a change to our mindset." However, resignation of the Vice-President Tin Aung Myint Oo, a former four-star general, and a close associate of retired dictator Than Shwe almost marks ending of the hardliner's role in the reformist government. He was considered as a leader of the hardline group in the government which is opposed to the liberal reforms of President Thein Sein. The development has been seen by many as another reformist move by President as he seeks to court the West and develop business ties and diplomatic ties after decades of estrangement.

Furthermore, appointment of a new negotiating team by President Thein Sein, to reach a ceasefire agreement with the KIO reflects a changing stance by the military, which is being involved in a newly restructured peace-negotiating process with the ethnic nationalities. The team would be led by Vice-President Sai Mauk Kham (who is a reformist and an ethnic Shan). Another liberal minded Rail Transportation Minister Aung Min, is also one of the chief negotiators of the team.

4.3.2 International Isolation

The new regime, although took steps to normalize its relation with the West, nevertheless, several thorny issues remain bilaterally, regionally and multilaterally. The issue of nuclear non-proliferation and growing closeness of Naypyidaw and Pyongyang has been a cause of growing concern for United States. However, the recent visit of the South Korean President in May 2012 has sent strong indications to North Korea. Relations between Seoul and Yangon are only now showing signs of recovery. Time and again US has also reminded India of its duty to speak out against human rights violation in Myanmar. It has asked India to engage the regime push for democracy and release of political prisoners. However, cautious optimism has characterised the response of the international community to the Aung San Suu Kyi meeting with the President Thein Sein and other leaders in 2011. The

US, United Kingdom, EU have become more pragmatic in its orientation and have launched a substantial review of their policy.

The reform agenda led by the new regime in Myanmar aims to convince the military that the process would be gradual and controlled and that the military's role as envisaged in the new Constitution would be respected. The leadership is trying hard to end its international isolation by promoting the democratic icon Nobel Laureate Aung San Suu Kyi. National League of Democracy (NLD) after participating in the by-elections on April 1, 2012 rejoined mainstream politics. The party has moved to revive and open new branch offices, reorganize its top brass and accept new member applications. The by-elections has been the biggest political test for the NLD since it last contested in elections in 1990, when it earned an overwhelming victory against the ruling military junta but was prevented from taking power. NLD remains a minority in the Parliament but its landslide victory inspired many citizens who are hoping for the country's full transition to democracy. The junta-backed USDP, although, is still the dominant force in the local politics.

As a victory for the new government seeking international legitimacy after a series of reform moves, Myanmar is to chair ASEAN in 2014, following an agreement between Southeast Asian leaders at their summit. The ASEAN leaders are now convinced about the significant changes and developments taking place in Myanmar and those changes have made it more conducive for Myanmar to carry out this responsibility. This would encourage the present government to step up the momentum for reforms. It has been alleged that by giving Myanmar the chance to chair ASEAN, the grouping was trying to ensure that the momentum of democratization in Myanmar was maintained, as it would put a bigger spotlight on the country, requiring it to be more open and transparent (*Jakarta Post* 2011).

Political change in Myanmar is being perceived as an opening of fresh opportunity to expand business by the so-called business tycoons—a result of crony capitalism of the military rule in Myanmar. Political and economic opening could lead United States and European Union to drop sanctions and allow Myanmar to compete in the global economy instead of relying on China for support. Furthermore, the new rapprochement marked by the US Secretary of State, Hillary Clinton's landmark visit to the country after more than fifty years of estrangement demonstrates that the process of reforms have gained momentum and recognition.[9] The United States eased certain financial restrictions on Myanmar in April 2012, to allow non-governmental groups to operate in the country as it undertakes democratic reforms. It would no longer restrict Americans from financial transactions in Myanmar if they are working for projects that "meet basic human needs" or promote democracy. Such projects include assistance to internally displaced people, delivery of clothes, food and medicine, as well as educational programs such as English-language instruction and anti-illiteracy efforts.

British Foreign Secretary William Hague, who visited Myanmar in more than 50 years, said that reforms undertaken so far by President Thein Sein raise hopes that democracy is within reach in the Southeast Asian nation.[10] British Prime Minister David Cameroon also made an announcement during his recent visit to Yangon and Naypidaw that his government would push for the suspension of European Union sanctions. The question however remains, how far and how fast the process of reform will develop (BBC 2012).

Minister of Foreign and European Affairs of France, Alain Juppe during his visit in January 2012 was convinced about the total agreement between the different authorities to move forward along the path of the regime's democratization and liberalization. The visit by French Foreign Minister has been a sign of Western approval of recent reforms by the new civilian government in Myanmar, after years of authoritarian rule (VOA 2012). In addition, the release of hundreds of political prisoners is seen as Myanmar's most significant step towards ending its isolation and securing the removal of European Union and US sanctions.

4.3.3 Political and National Reconciliation

The country needs to build up a political culture of democracy and public participation amidst the existing public apathy. Heralding a new kind of civilian leadership in the country, concrete steps for the reform agenda has acquired prominence. Parliamentary procedure which was completely stalled since last fifty years needs to be restored. The new Parliament has met thrice and various issues have come up for discussion such as social security, education, health care, environmental concerns and media reforms. Although power has been decentralized by the new Constitution, yet it needs to be utilized with a greater degree of caution because historically, the political culture of Myanmar is entrenched with authoritarian and paternalistic attitudes. For centuries, client-patron relationship and hierarchical social and political values have dominated political structure in Myanmar.

National reconciliation with the ethnic nationalities has to be more inclusive and political dialogue must be initiated to see how to guarantee these different ethnic minorities equal rights and conditions of economic development that are also as egalitarian as possible. Although the regime has witnessed transition, yet ethnic nationalities are unable to have their say in the governance. Addressing the issue of ethnic nationalities and resolving their decade-long conflict is one of the most important challenges facing the country. The counter insurgency methods used by the armed forces in the border areas have increased their alienation. Further, the pressure on ceasefire groups to join the controversial Border Guard Force (BGF) has aggravated their already existing grievances.[11] Recently, the use of Army's operation in Shan state has resulted in abuses against local citizens (EBO 2011: 2-3). Conflict has also erupted in Kachin State since May 2011.

In accordance with the 2008 Constitution, the power were decentralized to the region and state level, now each of these seven ethnic states having their own state legislature and governments. But in practical terms, after the 2010 elections, each of these structures of authorities is dominated by the members of USDP (TNI 2011: 2-3). The situation is thus, very far from the federal autonomy or self-governance as demanded by the ethnic nationalities. In addition, the overwhelming role of the military, in the legislature may help in promoting their own interest, rather than the local population. However, there seems to be little to suggest that the situation has improved for ethnic nationalities after elections. While some limited political space has been created, but it will hardly have any immediate impact.

The formation of the military alliance by the ethnic groups to assist each other in the event of attack by the army has posed a practical challenge before the new regime.[12] The use of violence in the Myawaddy region during November 2010 elections is a lesson which the new regime must always remember. In fact, it has been alleged that this was a part of the government's policy of eliminating ethnic opposition including ceasefire groups that have refused to be under its direct control as BGF, as required by the 2008 Constitution. Overcoming of sixty year old ethnic conflict will not be easy and the government will have to do a great deal to build the trust necessary to move beyond temporary ceasefires to resolve the underlying political issues (ICG 2011: 5).

The government has entered into a three step process for entering into a political dialogue with the ethnic nationalities (Mizzima 2012).[13] The first step is to agree a ceasefire between each armed group and the respective state or region government, which is seen as essential for building trust and confidence. The second step involves broader discussions between each group and the national government can begin to address other issues of concern, including socio-economic, cultural and political issues. The third stage is intended to bring together representatives of all armed groups and other stakeholders to discuss the shape of a lasting political agreement on ethnic issues. This would include issues such as constitutional change to give greater autonomy, provisions for greater resource sharing with ethnic communities, and the future integration and demobilisation of members of armed groups (ICG 2012: 5).

4.3.4 Human Rights Agenda

The government has shown willingness to target the human rights concern, but the issue of ongoing detention of more than 2000 political prisoners is a major challenge before the process of national reconciliation. One significant development in this regard has been the establishment of Myanmar Human Rights Commission on the recommendation of United Nations human rights envoy to Myanmar. But how far this independent body is going to be free and effective remains to be seen from the political space it would enjoy in the system of the newly established militarized regime.

Despite efforts to present itself as a legitimate and reform-oriented administration, the arbitrary punishment and human rights abuse continue in Myanmar (ALTSEAN 2011). Regime's repressive nature was revealed when an ex-army man was detained for ten years of imprisonment for dissemination of information to the dissident groups[14] (Democratic Voice of Burma 2011). Similarly, during the Martyr's Day ceremony former NLD member Pho Hlaoung was arrested under Immigration Act for attending the ceremony without approval of the authorities.

As a matter of concern, in the areas dominated by ethnic nationalities, armed conflict continues such as Kachin, Karen and Shan states. Here, military continues to target civilians during ongoing military offensives. Furthermore, reports of child soldiers and forced labour continue to remain serious issue of concern. Political prisoners have been denied rights under imprisonment with continued torture, inadequate medical care and ill-treatment. Besides, for the development of infrastructural projects, arbitrary confiscation of land and forced displacement has also led to serious political and human rights abuse in the country.

4.3.5 Economic Reforms

Although failure of regime performance in the economic front had delayed democracy in Myanmar, yet the new regime has taken all the possible steps for rebuilding the economy. President Thein Sein in his inaugural speech in the Parliament has focused on the 'economic might' for growth and development of the country. He emphasised on agricultural development as well as industrialization to transform country into a developed, rich one with a lot of employment opportunities and high per capita income. The new regime has invited a delegation from the International Monetary Fund (IMF) to visit in October to advise policymakers on how to tackle problems with the kyat currency, which has appreciated 20 per cent in a year, hurting farmers and exporters and bankrupting businesses. After months of inaction and simmering anger, the government in July 2011 cut taxes for exporters and has promised agriculture loans and price guarantees for millions of farmers, suggesting it may be concerned that any mishandling of bread and butter issues could see a repeat of bloody uprisings in 1988 and 2007 that were sparked by soaring inflation and fuel prices.

The country now after the 2010 elections is on a drive to attract investment, promoting tourism, timber, gemstones and its vast oil and gas reserves. In this regard, a "Special Economic Zone Law" was passed on January 27, 2011 to attract much-needed foreign capital to an economy held back by decades of sanctions and mismanagement. The new investment law follows a series of reforms undertaken over the past year, including the privatisation of hundreds of state assets, and plans to expand banking, telecommunications, shipping and agricultural sectors. Even Nobel laureate Suu Kyi has appealed for the support of the Burmese cause and establishment of a just political and economic order in Myanmar (Kyi 2011).

Nevertheless, major reforms are required by the new regime to restructure and re-invigorate the economy. It has to become more competitive before its entry into ASEAN FTA in 2015. Another major issue which needs to be focused is the rapid increase in the value of the local currency kyat. Myanmar's modest rate of growth at around 3 per cent is sufficient to finance the spending on health, education, and crucial infrastructure needed for transformational growth, but these revenues, unfortunately, are not utilized in constructive ways and have been channelized for arms and military infrastructure spending (Turnell 2011: 152). Its large fiscal deficit with a double digit inflation around 20 per cent is a matter of grave concern.

One of the primary challenges before the regime is Myanmar's rural financial system which is in poor shape. A vast majority of farmers are not able to access formal financing of any kind resulting in reliance on informal moneylenders whose high rate of interest results in an indebtedness cycle causing increasing landlessness. Transfer of technology and foreign direct investment beyond the resource extraction primarily in the field of construction of gas pipeline, mines and hydro-electric dams needs to be expanded. In addition, the quasi-privatization drive which began after selling off numerous state assets has been devoid of public tenders and transparency. They are primarily associated with regime connected conglomerates. Under this background, domestic hurdles in the economic field need to be targeted for implementing deep and lasting reforms. It has to really work hard for reversing the decades of economic mismanagement.

4.3.6 Battleground for Capitalist Penetration

Myanmar is seen by many investors as the next regional frontier market as businesses eye its huge natural resources, large population and strategic location between China and India. A spate of reforms have seen the international community roll back many of the tough sanctions put in place to punish a brutal junta that ruled with an iron fist until it was replaced by a quasi-civilian regime in 2010. Considered the last, large and untapped market in Asia, investors are eager to explore investments in Myanmar. As the sanctions have loosened, a rush for firms is looking to tap a potential 62 million consumers and a young workforce. It has turned out to be a new battleground for foreign investors and capitalist penetration. No one is talking about the human rights abuse and the hardship caused by the ethnic nationalities at the borders. Western intervention in Myanmar is moving away from humanitarian issues towards supporting capitalist penetration where MNCs from powerful countries are central players.

Many scholars have regarded it as the beginning of 'scramble for Myanmar' in the light of the changing stand of the Western powers and easing of the more than decade long sanction on the country (Singh 2012). Since 2011, Heads of states, diplomats, experts, business groups from Europe, America, Japan, Australia and South Korea have visited the country. Since then, various conferences, public events, official meetings and business forums are all geared towards fiscal liberalization. This has opened a new chapter in the history of Myanmar, where the country has become an economic battleground of capitalist penetration. This calls for the rise a critical left and strengthening of the civil society groups for fostering a critical social movement in the country. According to human rights groups, land battles are intensifying because companies tied to the military and business elite are rushing to grab land as the country emerges from five decades of isolation and opens its economy. Furthermore, political change sweeping through Myanmar means farmers and others are challenging land confiscations in ways that were unimaginable just a few years ago.

Global corporate giants from Coca-Cola to General Electric have already started their operation for a share of an expected economic boom in the so long isolated country. However, Parliament and the reformist President Thein Sein is working on the new investment law which seeks to introduce protectionist measures in the law, including that foreign firms would only be able to own up to a 50-per cent stake in joint ventures with local partners. The proposed law aims to put restriction on eleven sectors including farming, livestock breeding, fishing and agriculture—barred to foreign investors.

4.3.7 Environmental Hazards and Threat to Bio-diversity

Just as Myanmar seeks to emerge from dilapidated isolation and encourage investment in new infrastructure for electricity generation and transport to catch up with other Southeast Asian countries, it faces numerous environmental challenges and health hazards. "The 'development invasion' will speed up environmental destruction and is also likely to lead to more human rights abuses. As of now, the authoritarian regime and foreign companies that have invested in the country since the 1988 transition to a market-driven economy have destroyed the livelihoods of much of the population. The transition to a market economy has been crippled by the absence of the rule of law. Government policies and increasing globalization have lessened economic, social, cultural and environmental rights and contributed to an increase in poverty. Accountability, rule of law, freedom, transparency and security is what is required presently in Myanmar.

As foreign investments begin pouring in Myanmar in the wake of political reforms in 2010, Asia's last bastion of bio-diversity could be further lost and deteriorated. Virtually, non-existing environment laws and lack of a democratic social movement, has made environmental conservation a casualty of openness in Myanmar. Pro-democracy reformers and civil society groups associated with conservation have urged the government to put more stringent laws and safeguards into effect. The influx of investment threatens both ethnic minorities and the environment, according to a new report by the Burma Environment Working Group (BEWG). The report highlights how Myanmar lacks any meaningful frameworks on environmental protection and sustainable development that would enable citizens to take part in decision-making about their country's development, despite a recent transition to a military-dominated parliamentary political system. Unless a sound policy framework for environmental protection and sustainable development are in place to ensure that investment does not lead to unnecessary destruction of the natural environment and local livelihoods, Myanmar's environment will continue to be a source of conflict.

The environment activists called for new and existing investors to stop immediately all project-related works—especially in responsive states all over Myanmar—until satisfactory safeguards are in place to ensure investment does not lead to unnecessary destruction of the natural environment and local livelihoods. The new measures are brought in to ensure sustainable development and multi-ethnic participation.

In this regard, mention may be particularly made of the suspension of the Myitsone dam in September 2011, which was being constructed on the Irrawaddy River in the northern state of Kachin in Myanmar with the help of Chinese company.[15]

All's said and done, the new democratic regime in Myanmar is just born and it is taking its baby-steps. In this stage, it has to face a number of teething troubles. It still has a long way to go from infancy to adolescence. It is hoped that as it moves forward in its growth and maturity, these problems would be overpowered by the emergence of a more open and matured democracy in future. President Thein Sein in his recent address to the Parliament has promised that reforms would continue but "democratization is in its infancy."

Notes

1. The National League for Democracy (NLD), the main opposition party to Myanmar's ruling military junta, was disbanded on 6 May, 2010 because it had refused to register for the upcoming elections in November 2010. The party's Central Executive Committee voted unanimously not to take part in the elections, to protest against elections rules, especially the one that requires it to expel its leader because of prior convictions (particularly Aung San Suu Kyi).
2. Mrs. Clinton is the first US Secretary of State to visit Myanmar since John Foster Dulles visited in 1955.
3. For details see *New Light of Myanmar,* 17 March 2011, p. 12.
4. To quote President Thein Sein,

   "Regarding the health sector, we will improve quality of the hospitals opened over past two decades and skills of medical staff. In addition, we will improve the quality of rural health centres and medical staff. In the process, we will work together with international organizations including the UN, INGOs, and NGOs. We have a plan to promulgate necessary laws to standardize the health care services of private health centres. We also have a plan to set up a health care system covering the participation of the State, the people and altruistic organizations to beef up community health care. We will work more closely with international organizations in pursuit of the national projects on control and prevention of the three diseases: AIDS, tuberculosis and malaria".
5. To quote President Thein Sein,

   "Regarding the education sector, the 24 regions for special development have been established with universities and colleges so that local youths can pursue higher education in their regions or states. Rural areas have seen a massive number of basic education schools. In order to promote the nation's education standard to the international level, we will practise free compulsory primary education system, improve the standards of present universities, colleges, and high, middle and primary schools, provide more teaching aids, sharpen the abilities and improve the socio-economic status of educational staff, and increase the enrolment rates in middle and high schools. In that regard, we will work in cooperation with international organizations including the UN, INGOs, and NGOs. We will promulgate necessary laws for private education schools. Moreover, we will provide stipends for higher education abroad and stipends for outstanding students at home."

6. To quote President Thein Sein,

   "Another task we will have to implement is environmental conservation. In that regard, we will pay serious attention to conservation of forests and woodlands and take measures in various sectors to reduce air and water pollution, control dumping of industrial waste and conserve wildlife. We will lay down a new policy in which we will work for economic development in parallel with environmental conservation. We will mobilize participation of the people and social organizations in the tasks for environmental conservation and create renewable energy at low cost. We will review and amend laws and enact new laws on environmental conservation".

7. Reuters (2011)

8. Based on Harn Yawnghwe's visit to Myanmar from 20-28 October, 2011. URL: http://www.shanland.org/index.php?option=com_content&view=article&id=4151:harn-yawnghwe-winds-up-fruitful-tour-of-home-country&catid=85:politics&Itemid=266

9. Mrs Clinton is the first US Secretary of State to visit Myanmar in December 2011 since John Foster Dulles visited in 1955.

10. William Hague visited the country in January 2012.

11. All ceasefire groups were asked to form BGF by September 1, 2010.

12. The military alliance was formed in January 2010 by Kachin Independence Army (KIA) the Karen National Liberation Army (armed wing of KNU) and the Chin National Army (armed wing of Chin National Front -CNF)

13. Based on the President Thein Sein's 1 March 2012 address to the Union Parliament.

14. Nay Myo Zin has been sentenced to 10 years in prison under the Electronics Act. He was later charged for allegedly making contacts with Voice of America (VOA) news agency's reporter Rodney Nyein (also known as) Thaung Nyein [who conducted radio talk shows with former army officials] and also taking part in an exile-political group known as

Patriotic War Veterans of Burma and writing articles under pseudonyms Shwe Bann and Nyi Toe Nyein [on political blogs].

15. Groups usually positioned against each other across ethnic, religious or political lines on this issue appear united. Burmese or Kachin; existing regime or opposition; religious or secular; Christian or Buddhist; pro-West, pro-military or pro-China political factions—almost all agree that the government was right to shelve the project at the source of the Irrawaddy River (Hui 2012).

Chapter 5

Media vis-à-vis the Authoritarian State in Myanmar

5.1 AUTHORITARIAN MEDIA REGIME IN MYANMAR

During the Parliamentary Democracy period between 1948 and 1962, Myanmar experienced relative freedom of press and media. Writers and artists enjoyed almost total freedom of expression. As many as three dozen newspapers, including English, Chinese and Hindi dailies, existed between 1948 and 1962. But this ended with the military coup in 1962 led by General Ne Win. The situation changed in 1962 when the military seized power. All newspapers were nationalized and a Press Scrutiny Board created to enforce strict censorship on all forms of printed matter. Since then, censorship and self-censorship have become commonplace in Myanmar.

During the period of military rule, which exists till today, free expression and the right to criticize government policy were gradually suppressed. In August 1962, The Printers' and Publishers' Registration Act was promulgated by the military regime. Under this act, all printers and publishers were required to register and to present two copies of all proposed books to the Press Scrutiny Board (PSB). Additionally, very few social scientists have been allowed to conduct research in Myanmar and journalists are limited in how long they can stay and where they can go. At the same time, the Burmese scholars and authors inside the country have not been able to write openly about such matters because of strict censorship rules (Fink 2001: 4-5).

The Printers' and Publishers' Central Registration Board, in July 1975, issued an 11-point guideline that basically forbids all writings against the "socialist" state, its policies, and its actions. After the present military regime came into power in 1988, the Press Scrutiny Board, far from being disbanded, was strengthened (*Mizzima News* 2008). Every writer, every poet, every cartoonist is always ruled by the fear that what he or she has written will not get passed the censor. Apart from newspapers and magazines, the radio and television are also under the tight control of the military government (Luwarso 2000). The New Light of Myanmar is a total propaganda machine for the government. Foreign journalists are rarely allowed entry visas to the country and the military intelligence units of the government constantly monitor those who are admitted. The state-run media has been forced to show the courage which is favourable to SPDC and the USDA. They have been provided with facts and figures about infrastructure—roads, bridges, hospitals so as to create a positive response in the minds of its supporters (Bowman 2007: 9-10). Various non-state media has also been bribed for running coverage favourable to the SPDC. Various foreign media agencies such as Radio Free Asia, Voice of America and Democratic Voice of Burma have been critically circumscribed.

In Myanmar today, aggressive state censorship works in concert with techniques of survellience and intimidation to stifle political debate and suppress criticism of government policies. At the same time, a relentless rhetoric pervades the state-owned news media promoting an official vision of the "Myanmar nation" (Leehey 2005: 176). The ruling military authorities seek extensive control over public discourse. The following section looks at the various phases in the evolution of mass media in Myanmar.

5.1.1 Press Censorship in BSPP Era

Some form of the present-day censorship apparatus has been in place in Myanmar for over four decades. The main legal instrument of censorship—the Printers' and Publishers' Registration Law (PPRL)—was promulgated in 1962, shortly after the military coup that brought General Ne Win to power.

Before Ne Win, during the parliamentary era, in the 1950s, Myanmar had one of the freest presses in Asia. There were more than thirty newspapers in several languages published in several cities, with editorial positions reflecting a broad range of political opinions. Prime Minister, U Nu did maintain a Press Review Department (PRD), but it only monitored and did not directly censor publications. After 1962, conditions for publishing changed markedly.

The military rule under Revolutionary Council directly attacked the media. Several newspapers were closed down, including the English language daily *The Nation*. Several editors and journalists were arrested apparently for printing criticism of government policies. The Revolutionary Council started an official state newspaper *Loktha Pyithu Nayzin*, with an English version called *The Working Peoples Daily*.

By 1964, all private newspaper were nationalised and brought under the direct control of Ministry of Information and Broadcasting. It was proclaimed that they would have full freedom of expression within the limits of Burmese Way of Socialism (Allot 1981: 18). All newspapers along with other mass media such as radio and later television became mouthpiece of BSPP. During this period, the government exercised control over publishers also by limiting the allocation of subsidised paper, as paper was short in supply under the centralised socialist economy.

Private publishing of books and non-news periodicals continued but under a strict new regulatory framework. The 1962, PPRL established a Press Scrutiny Board (PSB) to control the books and periodicals. Unlike PRD, which had simply monitored publications, the PSB was vested with extensive power to prohibit the distribution of any material it considered unacceptable. The Board not only supervised the language and contents of the printed wok but also determined the number of copies that could be legally printed.

The PPRL has been amended several times, mostly to expand its scope. In practice, the procedures of the PSB have encouraged self-censorship. Throughout 1960s and 1970s, works on politics, economics and religion had to be submitted before printing in typed manuscript form. The PSB often required changes or deletions which had to be carried out. If a work was banned, the entire print run had to be destroyed. Therefore, only few publishers could afford to take risks especially because of prohibitive cost of paper. Small book-rental shops running from the front rooms of private houses also became widespread during this period because of the high cost and general scarcity of the reading materials.

The writers and publishers were raising objections by mid-1970s to the system. In 1977, the government instituted new pre-publication scrutiny shortly after the publication of *Hpaung-ga-za Maung Maung*, a book with anti-government themes (Allot 1981: 34). Under the new instructions , all book-length texts had to be submitted as manuscript in twenty typed copies. Pre-publication censorship entailed new hardships: writers had to contend personally with the board's many demands for alterations, and it could take months, even years, to receive final approval to publish (Leehey 2005: 178). One of the most important problems for the writers and publishers during this period was to determine what the PSB would reject. Its decision often seemed to be quite arbitrary. In 1975, the Ministry of Home and Religious Affairs issued a memorandum laying out principles for the censorship board to follow, which were almost vague and sweeping. Virtually, any piece of writing could be objected to under one or another of the principles (Allot 1993).[1]

Difficulties involved in publishing book length works gave rise to monthly literary magazines. These became important forum for serious writings in 1970 and 1980s. These magazines featured short-stories, serialised novels, general interest and foreign news features, cartoons and poems. It was easy to remove these short-stories and poems from the magazines, if at all, censorship was required.

5.1.2 Media Freedom: Interregnum during 1988

When the anti-government demonstrations swept the country in August 1988, many unlicensed publications sprang up, carrying reports of the protests and interviews with the opposition leaders. Magazine articles criticized of the government and economy were allowed to appear. There were indications that restrictions on press might be easing. Even the state-run newspaper seemed to be printing accurate information without intervention (Leehey 2005: 178). All the workers were out demonstrating in support of four demands: the resignation of the government; the formation of an interim government; the holding of multiparty elections; and the right to publish freely (Allot 1993). The official newspapers that reappeared after the break were much changed—they were reporting more accurately what was actually happening. At this point the first unofficial news sheets also began to appear, with much fuller detail, with graphic, even lurid photographs, and containing many expressions of personal opinion, as people lost their fear and became prepared to speak out, sensing that the changes they were asking for might be within their grasp. Nearly one hundred such unofficial publications have been recorded (*ibid.*). The earliest of these is dated August 27, the latest September 21, 1988. It also became possible for private individuals and organizations to obtain licenses to publish new magazines. They all advocated democratic movement and people's power while criticizing and ridiculing the BSPP and its leaders (Than 2002: 148).

Journalistic activity continued to increase in intensity and effectiveness, almost as if the free, unofficial publications were spurring the official press to give more accurate information. And indeed this is what government employees working in radio, TV, and the press had just gone on strike for: the right to put out accurate information about internal events. They knew, as everyone else knew, that for years the picture they had been presenting to the Burmese public had borne little relation to reality. In the exciting atmosphere of what was hailed as the Burmese version of glasnost, they too wanted to be able to speak freely and truthfully. The official press began to carry numerous pictures of peaceful demonstrators marching in Rangoon, lists of their demands and, more worrying, accounts of widespread looting on a massive scale, with shocking incidents of mob revenge. As yet, the press contained little analysis or comment. Indeed, some of the leaders and feature articles were staggeringly irrelevant, as if they had been written to order months in advance. The unofficial press, however, carried all this news and much more: dramatic photographs of the demonstrations taken from *Asiaweek*, long interviews with opposition leaders including Daw Aung San Suu Kyi, feature articles about the British Broadcasting Service's World Service, and about how elections are conducted in Western democracies. Most important, there were courageous personal statements by older Burmese journalists, silenced for so long, of their reactions to events and to Dr. Maung Maung's speeches. They wrote about the abuses of the present system, about the desperate need to find a solution to the nation's problems, and about the need for the army and the people to work together.

This was a short-lived affair and was abruptly terminated by the military coup of 18 September 1988. The brief period of press freedom came to a close when General Saw Maung seized power. The honeymoon period of press freedom, thus, lasted less than one month. On September 16, amid more bloody confrontations in which the military brutally slaughtered many civilians (again, estimates vary), the government ordered all military, police, and public servants to resign from the Burmese Socialist Programme Party—many civil servants had already done so—and to return to work. On September 18, the army seized power from the government of the country, and General Saw Maung became the chairman of a new governing body, the State Law and Order Restoration Council (SLORC). On September 19 and 20, there were no official newspapers, but by September 21, the old-style *Lok-tha Pyei-thu Nei-zin* (*Working People's Daily*) was back—a newspaper that contained little in the way of real news and nothing in the way of objective comment. In April 1993, the SLORC decided that, in order to shed the paper's socialist image, it should be renamed *Myanma Alin* (*The New Light of Myanmar*), the name of one of Myanmar's leading nationalist newspapers in the 1920s and 1930s.

5.1.3 Press Freedom and Censorship: 1988 and Beyond

During the heady months of August and September 1988, many regular contributors to Myanmar's numerous monthly magazines were drawn into helping with the numerous unofficial publications, with the result that many magazines temporarily ceased publication. After the SLORC's seizure of power, a considerable number of leading writers decided to continue their political activities and took up functions in the emerging political parties, which left them little time for ordinary writing. At the same time all "socialist" journals and magazines put out under the aegis of the Burmese Socialist Programme Party ceased publication. Prices were rising and publishing became more expensive.

The PSB, however, although a creation of the Burmese Way to Socialism, far from being disbanded, was strengthened; it tightened its supervision and continued to censor all publications in accordance with its previous guidelines, merely dropping the word "socialist." If anything, the PSB now appeared to writers in Myanmar to pursue ever more restrictive policies, becoming extremely sensitive to hidden meanings and democratic ideas in stories, poems, and articles. With each fresh instance of censorship, writers and magazine editors would be forced to alter their future approach.

There was a blacklist, supplied to the PSB by the military intelligence, of authors and people whose work may not be published at all, and whose names may not even appear in print. Neither the work, nor even the name of someone currently in jail may appear in print. And the same restriction also applied to some (but not all) released writers, for example, Daw San San Nwe, one of whose stories appears in this collection. Others who were outspoken in their support of the prodemocracy movement such as U Pe Thein (whose gentle humor and wisdom makes him Myanmar's best-loved cartoonist), have been totally banned from appearing in print. For such people this means that they have been prevented from earning their living in the way that they had been doing before.

In March 1993, these restrictions seem to have been lifted in certain cases, but not all. An example of the great harm done to the literary life of Myanmar is the case of an anthology of short-stories that was published in December 1991, issued in memory of an outstanding woman writer, MoMo (Inya), who had died suddenly in March 1990. The book, *The Best Short Stones of the 80s*, is a collection of previously published works and included the work of thirty-seven carefully selected authors. However, in between the time of choosing the authors and that of printing the book and submitting it to the PSB, three of the selected authors were arrested. The result was that the publisher was forced to rip out their three stories from the already printed and bound book. The author's names also had to be blanked out, using silver ink, from the table of contents. A fourth story, about a noted political figure, Thakin Kodaw Hmaing, was also torn out, since he had, for unclear reasons, become a persona non grata. Even more pettily, throughout the volume, wherever a story was listed as having first appeared in *Pe-hpu-hlwa*, a magazine which had been shut down by the SLORC, this name also had to be wiped out. The final assault on the volume, before it was permitted to go on sale, was to the cover: an image of MoMo's head, embossed on a medallion, had to be covered over with a strip of gold paper, because the PBS feared that the Myanmar's reading public might be reminded of Daw Aung San Suu Kyi and the Nobel Peace Prize she had recently been awarded. This volume was an exceptional publishing venture, presenting as it did a carefully chosen selection of the best short-stories of the 1980s in a large-format, highly-produced volume costing an unusually expensive seventy-five kyats. Future generations of Burmese readers will doubtless decry the mutilations to the volume at the PSB's behest.

As well as the blacklist, there were a new range of topics that may not be touched upon in non-government-sponsored writing. (The government, however, reserves the right to write on all topics.) Off-limits topics include: democracy; human rights; politics; the events of 1988; senior government officials; the BSPP (the word "socialist" was actually blanked out of the phrase "socialist realism" in the foreword by Daw Amar to a book of short-stories in 1992); the Nobel Prize or anything that might bring Daw Aung San Suu Kyi to mind (a story in which the heroine's name was "Ma Su" had to be ripped out of a magazine); criticism of the SLORC or of military personnel; "immorality" such as references to two unmarried people living together; prostitution in Myanmar; and any other topics determined unsuitable by the PSB.

The interference with an author's right to decide about his own work starts at the petty level of spelling. For example, the word do ("we" or "our," as in do-bama, meaning "we Burmese," an evocative usage), may only be used by those in power, while ordinary writers must just use the spelling to (which has no nationalist overtones). The interference also affects such final decisions about books as the cover design: too much red is not permitted, boys must not be wearing trousers, young couples should not be shown kissing. A further indignity endured by authors is that every book and magazine is obliged to carry on its first or second page a series of government slogans, starting with:

> The Three Main National Causes are:
> non-disintegration of the Union,
> non-disintegration of national solidarity, and
> the continuing maintenance of national sovereignty;
> It ended with the statement:
> The emergence of the state constitution is the chief duty of all citizens.

Sometimes the SLORC's inclination to put words into writers' and editors' mouths goes further—magazine editors have frequently had pressure put on them to publish government-sponsored articles intended to foster the reader's national pride and to preserve traditional Burmese culture in the face of growing Western influence.

Soon after the announcement of the award of the Nobel Peace Prize to Daw Aung San Suu Kyi in October 1991, the PSB instituted an objectionable new rule by which authors have to submit biographical details together with their manuscript. The form requires them to state if they have engaged in political activity or if they have served a prison sentence, in which case their work may well be rejected. Editors of magazines are also required to countersign these forms, with the aim of flushing out banned authors who are writing under a pseudonym. Political acceptability, rather than literary merit, is what enables a work to get into print, and editors of monthly literary magazines are increasingly embarrassed by the changes they are obliged to ask writers to make, especially in cases of senior and respected authors.

The PSB would decide that certain items are to be inked over or that certain pages are to be ripped out. In this case, the offending item must be blotted out with silver ink or ripped out of every single copy. Any story, poem, cartoon, passage, or word not allowed by the PSB had to be eliminated before the work can go on sale. This was done by ripping out pages, by gluing them together, by inking over with silver paint, or by sticking opaque tape over the offending item. This ripping and blanking out was carried out by the publisher, following the instructions of the PSB. After the pages had been torn out, they were sent back to the PSB which counted them (to ensure that none have been left in or distributed separately), and then destroyed them. The PSB "knew" how many copies have been printed, and this destruction meant that censored authors were often unable to receive the ripped-out pages of their stories.

5.1.4 Re-emergence of Private Media in 1990s

Under the new regime of SLORC in 1990s, the private print industry considerably expanded—both qualitatively and quantitatively to cater for the demands of the economy. A new generation of magazines and journals that focus on economic matters proliferated in the early 1990s in line with the opening of the economy (Than 2008: 148). Government agencies dealing with trade commerce and tourism also produced similar publications. However, by 2000 only few of them survived. The state bureaucracy and the publishing industry were particularly intertwined in the area of licensing (Leehey 2005: 183). In the early 1990s, the authorities issued a number of new publishing licenses to government departments and agencies so that these offices could develop sources of revenue to subsidise employees low salaries. Furthermore, liberalization reduced the paper cost and more print quality paper became available. This further opened up opportunities for small-scale entrepreneurial ventures in publishing. New publishing houses were established and an array of new periodicals appeared, including monthly magazines and small weekly and biweekly papers. There were popular weeklies and monthlies concerned with astrology, numerology, and the supernatural topics of perennial fascination in Myanmar that were prohibited from print in the socialist period.

5.2 EXILED MEDIA AND THE INTERNET: BLESSING IN DISGUISE

"While journalism in Myanmar is in a deep coma, it is not dead" (Zaw 2002). But there are many topics considered off-limits by Burmese media, which primarily serve as the government's voice. The government's press scrutiny board will not allow the media to publish news that could in any way reflect badly on the regime. Although virtually none of the media inside Myanmar could elude state censorship, a vigorous exiled press does provide access to a wider variety of information sources to those Burmese who can afford satellite dishes to obtain their broadcasts. An estimated one million Burmese, mostly living in urban centres have access to such services (HRW 2008). International news services such as British Broadcasting Centre (BBC)—Burmese Service, Radio Free Asia (RFA), Voice of America (VOA) and Norway-based Democratic Voice of Burma (DVB) provide critical information to those who can afford. Thus, news-starved Burmese tune in to shortwave radio stations such as the BBC, VOA or the Washington-based Radio Free Asia (RFA) for alternative news. These radio stations have gained popularity because the government's news dispatches are no longer reliable for the general public. And journalists are wary of government intrusion, too.

With the rise of the Internet as a widely available resource in the early 1990s, several pro-democracy Burmese expatriates began to communicate over an electronic mailing list called seasia-l, which was used for discussions about Southeast Asia. In 1994, Burma Net emerged as the first source of online news about Myanmar, particularly information about human rights abuses collected primarily from newspapers in Thailand. It remains one of the major aggregators for news about Myanmar. A grant from the Soros Foundation provided a boost to this early effort, which quickly attracted the attention of many Burmese expatriates and Myanmar sympathizers.

During the early years of the Internet, the Burmese government likely did not foresee that the Internet would become an alternative news source that would also launch a new breed of dissenters: digital activists. In the mid-1990s, online news sites dedicated to the promotion of democracy in Myanmar began to emerge. This was a significant step forward compared to earlier online news groups and mailing lists, which only collected materials from mainstream media sources. Websites such as Irrawaddy (www.irrawaddy.org), Mizzima News (www.mizzima.com) and Democratic Voice of Burma (www.dvb.no) which were established by Burmese journalists living in exile began to gradually generate independent news about Myanmar. Many of these sites were based in Thailand and were closely affiliated with pro-democracy movements.

The Internet allowed users to become creators of content instead of just consumers of information. With no easy way to stop the information flow in cyberspace, the military government began to actively promote its own views online. A military representative regularly transmitted the regime's official statements on BurmaNet and the soc.culture.burma newsgroup, and also sometimes participated in online discussions and debates. In 1996, the government stepped up its efforts to curb production of unauthorized online media content with the establishment of the Computer Science Development Law, which prohibited ownership of a computer, modem, or fax machine without prior approval of the Ministry of Communications. It further prescribed a prison sentence of seven to fifteen years for violators. The law also established harsh measures against the establishment of computer networks without government approval. The government also created its own online platforms to compete with BurmaNet, including its own electronic mailing list, Myanmar Net. As one might expect it was strictly moderated and presented official news and policy statements—many lifted from the state-controlled newspaper *New Light of Myanmar*.

Two government websites, myanmar.com and myanmar-information.net, were also established and regularly provided government-approved information about Myanmar. The first is an official government portal with links to national government agencies and newspapers. The second is a daily compilation of news items coming from various government sources. These sites are also used to address international accusations against the regime. Some believe that the Internet is used by the junta to "misinform, divide and intimidate." According to an activist based in Ireland: Before the Net, the regime had no real voice in the world. Now, it has its own platform to woo naive potential tourists and provide information for business interests. The multilingual www.myanmar.com attempts to paint Myanmar as a peaceful, beautiful, welcoming place. Most people will not be fooled by the blatant disinformation, but inevitably it gets through to some.

The senior leadership has instructed ministers to bombard the state-run media with facts and figures about infrastructure, in the belief that if the population is aware of the number of roads, hospitals and bridges built since 1988, they will support the SPDC. As part of this public relations drive, Information Minister, Brigadier-General Kyaw Hsan, revived regular press conferences and took to bribing or forcing the non-state media into running coverage positive to the SPDC. He also increased attacks on the vernacular radio stations beyond his control (the BBC, Radio Free Asia, Voice of America and the Democratic Voice of Burma), on whom the majority of the population relies for domestic news.

As part of its media campaign since 2005, the SPDC has intensified its public attacks on anyone it perceives as a possible political challenge such as the NLD and the '1988 students'. According to Bowman (2007), "the number of articles in the state-run media seeking to discredit the NLD as 'Western stooges' and 'axe-handles' and the verbal attacks on individuals increased in frequency and rancour".

The Saffron Revolution resulted in a major online international campaign. These include protesters in thirty countries and almost one hundred cities across the globe including Sydney, Ottawa, Paris, Hong Kong, Delhi, London, New York, and Washington D.C. Protestors in each city organized peaceful rallies in strategic locations to increase awareness of the monk-led revolution in Myanmar. The Global Day of Action was organized almost completely online. This included the more than three hundred thousand members of the Facebook group 'Support the Monks' Protest.' To drum up support and awareness among bloggers before the event, an International Bloggers' Day for Burma, a 'blog blackout' day, was organized on October 4. Bloggers that took part did not write posts that day and displayed banners on their blogs with only the words 'Free Burma.'

Internet slowdowns, cyber attacks and tampering have been a common instrument of the military regime. Journalists who collaborate with the exiled Burmese media and bloggers had to bear the brunt of the authorities, particularly since the 2007 Saffron Revolution and the international outcry which followed the mass circulation of images of the ensuing crackdown. The authorities made use of the unabashed use of a particularly repressive law adopted in 2004, the Electronic Transactions Law, to regulate the Internet, TV and radio. This law notably prohibits the import, possession, and use of a modem without official permission, under penalty of 7-15 year prison sentence for "undermining state security, national unity, culture, the national economy and law and order (articles 33-38)."[2] The 1996 Computer Science Development Law bans any information posted on the Internet that in the junta's view may undermine the interests and security of the country. According to the law, "Whoever imports or keeps in possession or utilizes any type of computer network without the prior sanction of the Ministry of Communications, Posts and Telegraphs shall, on conviction be punished with imprisonment for a term which may extend from a minimum of 7 years to a maximum of 15 years and may also be liable to a fine" (article 32).[3] The 1996 Television and Video Act has penalties of up to three years jail term for "copying, distributing, hiring or exhibiting video tape that has no video censor certificate (articles 32-36)."[4]

A drastic slowdown in Internet connections was noted in early October, more than a month before the elections, indicating the authorities' resolve to tighten their control over information. Just a few days prior to the legislative elections, the Burmese Internet network experienced a massive cyber attack. The attacks began around 25 October 2010 and gradually increased in number and severity, causing the country to be regularly disconnected from the web for several days. They continued to occur until the elections were over, which made it extremely difficult for journalists and netizens to transmit videos and photos and to do their jobs (based on Report of Reporters Without Borders).

Table 5.1: Myanmar Newspapers and News Media—National and Foreign

	Myanmar—Broadcast News Media	
National	MRTV 3	English TV Also Burmese
Foreign	Burma FM	English Radio
Foreign	DVB	English Radio TV
Foreign	DVB	Burmese Radio TV
	Myanmar—Magazine News Media	
Foreign	Irrawaddy	English
Foreign	Irrawaddy	Burmese
	Myanmar—Newspaper News Media	
National	Kyehmon	Burmese Site 1
National	Kyehmon	Burmese Site 2
National	Kyehmon	Burmese
	Myanmar Newspapers and News Media—Local (Yangon)	
Yangon	7 Days News Journal	MYA
Yangon	Kyehmon	MYA Site 1
Yangon	Kyehmon	MYA Site 1

Yangon	Myanmar Alin	MYA
Yangon	Myanmar Times	ENG
Yangon	Myanmar Times	MYA
Yangon	New Light of Myanmar	ENG Site 1
Yangon	New Light of Myanmar	ENG Site 2
Yangon	Yangon FM	ENG
Yangon	Yangon Globe	ENG Radio
Myanmar—Internet News Media		
National	Myanmar	English
National	Myanmar Disest	English
Foreign	Big News Network	English
Foreign	Burma Daily	English
Foreign	Burma Net News	English
Foreign	Burma Project Southeast Asia Initiative	English
Foreign	Initiative	Burmese
Foreign	Burma Today	English
Foreign	EIN News	English
Foreign	Index Mundi	English
Foreign	IRIN	English
Foreign	Kao Wao	English
Foreign	Mizzima	Burmese
Foreign	Mizzima	English
Foreign	Myanma Thadin	Burmese
Foreign	Myanma Thadin	English
Foreign	Myanmar News	English
Foreign	Narinjara	Burmese
Foreign	Narinjara	English
Foreign	News Now	English
Foreign	Topix Burma	English
Foreign	Yahoo	English

5.3 THE NEW REGIME AND MEDIA

Myanmar's once watertight censorship board has in recent months undertaken reforms. The amendment to the country's press laws in March to allow the majority of non-news journals to bypass pre-censorship was accompanied by the announcement that two Thailand-based dailies, the *Bangkok Post* and *The Nation*, will soon be allowed to hit news-stands in Yangon. These events have helped to maneuvour the carefully crafted image of a government loosening its manaever on the media as it moves steadily towards democratic reform. President Thein Sein mentioned in his inaugural speech that media is the fourth pillar of the nation and media laws need to be amended in line with the provisions of the Constitution and that 'it is getting more and more developed'. The Information and Broadcasting Minister has also highlighted that there would be more freedom of press and the government has offered strong indications that it may relax media restrictions. Under the proposed changes, coverage on mostly benign subjects, including sports and entertainment, would no longer have to pass through the office of the censor before hitting news-stands.

In September 2011, pro-democracy icon Aung San Suu Kyi published her first article in the Burmese media for 23 years on the front page of *Pyithu Khit News Journal*, while Messenger News also ran an exclusive interview with the Nobel Laureate as its cover story. Pyithu Khit (People's Era) was permitted by the Burmese censorship board—the Press Scrutiny and Registration Division under the Ministry of Information—to publish Suu Kyi's article entitled "Holiday-1". It also carried a piece by one of her close aides—veteran journalist Win Tin's old article on Suu Kyi's father Aung San. For the last 23 years, even Suu Kyi's name or any symbols indirectly referring to her—such as "the lady," "the mother" or "the rose"—was banned in publications. This move is a part of the recent relaxation of control over media, seen as part of the new, nominally civilian government's effort to reach out to the democratic opposition in a bid to win greater international recognition. As Myanmar enters a new political phase, the international community should seize the opportunity to encourage greater openness and reforms.

In August, the *Irrawaddy* became available online in Myanmar for the very first time. In some ways, these are good days for Myanmar's exiled journalists. Based in Chiang Mai, a sleepy city of ancient Buddhist temples in northern Thailand, the *Irrawaddy* saw its Burmese-language website get a record 222,270 unique visitors in January, up nearly 40% year on year. Myanmar is now home to the outlet's second biggest audience after Singapore, with 42,250 monthly visitors. A wall featuring the *Irrawaddy*'s past covers in its small offices above a Thai-massage school bears testament to the coverage that's made the publication vital reading over the years. "Where are sanctions taking Burma?" asks one from May 2001. "Burma's long road to reconciliation," reads a January 2004 issue.

Meanwhile, Oslo-based Democratic Voice of Burma (DVB), which produces three hours of daily satellite TV, as well as radio and online content, from a small three-storeyed office on the outskirts of Chiang Mai, is also flourishing. DVB began in 1992 as a radio station operating out of Oslo, Norway, with a rudimentary bureau in the Manerplaw region of Karen state. Since then it has gradually expanded, and in 2005 became the first non-state media group to broadcast television inside Myanmar. Its work during the September 2007 monk-led uprising formed the focus of the Oscar-nominated Myanmar VJ documentary. The film depicted the risks involved in filming undercover in Myanmar at a time when the junta held a zero-tolerance policy towards independent media. At one point, 17 video journalists working for DVB were in prison in Myanmar, some serving sentences of more than 60 years, but all were freed in an amnesty of political prisoners in January this year.

DVB estimates it now reaches 5 million to 10 million people across its various platforms, with its Burmese-language website getting 20,000 visitors a day and the English section pulling in 8,000 more. Exiled reporters working for the Democratic Voice of Burma will be granted visas to carry out assignments inside the country for the first time since the organisation was founded nearly two decades ago. Long a target of intimidation and punishment by the Burmese regime, DVB has been forced to operate from offices based in Norway, Thailand and India. Staff who travel to the country have risked lengthy prison sentences, while its network of in-country journalists have carried out their work underground. But Information Minister Kyaw Hsan has said that criminalisation of the exiled media group will begin to ease, starting with permission for staff living outside of the country to enter on five-day journalist visa.

Indeed, journalists are still wary of the state. Myanmar's military rulers have a long history of persecuting independent reporters and ranked among the world's five worst jailers of the press for the past four consecutive years, according to the Committee to Protect Journalists. Despite unprecedented reforms in 2011 and promises of a new, less restrictive media law this year, the country's censorship rules remain among the strictest in the world, and foreign and exiled media personnel are still denied working visas. "Even if the media laws are amended, we can expect to face both soft and self-censorship in the future," says Thiha Saw, chief editor of a Myanmar-based news weekly called *Open News*. "We need the Burmese exile media to tell the truth and print the stories that journals inside Myanmar cannot." Myanmar's President Thein Sein has vowed to build on the sweeping reforms it began after 2010.

Mizzima, a Myanmar-focused news agency founded in India in 1998 with offices in New Delhi and Chiang Mai, has decided to move its operations to Myanmar and participate in meetings organized by the government to redraft the country's media laws. Founding Editor Soe Myint is reticent to discuss its current legal status and office locations, but insists the outlet wants to be part of the process from inside the country. "We believe that with the openings by the government, we are able to work," he said in a phone interview from Rangoon. Khuensai Jaiyen, editor of the *Shan Herald*, a newspaper reporting on Myanmar's Shan minority, said he plans to send a third of his staff into the country, adopting a "one foot in, one foot out" strategy. "It's not the time to put all the eggs in the basket," he said (Jackson 2012).

The mainstays of the exiled-media scene, the *Irrawaddy* and DVB, have adopted a similarly cautious approach. Although Aung Zaw has been to Rangoon and a couple of reporters are heading into the country on assignment, there are no plans for relocation. "After 2015, we will know which direction the country's going and how safe we are," he says. DVB announced in March 2012 that its exiled reporters would be granted visas to carry out assignment inside the country for the first time since the organization was founded nearly two decades ago.

In some ways, rapprochement threatens the very existence of exile media groups, most of which rely on donor funding. Among journalists in Chiang Mai, there is a pronounced fear that the promise of reform will cause donations to dry up. "Exile media are trying to redefine themselves, and their future will depend on a continuation of democratic reform," says Lars Bestle, head of the International Media Support's Asia program, which funds outlets like Mizzima. Some donors, like the U.S.-based National Endowment for Democracy (NED), which spends around $750,000 on independent multi-language media in Myanmar across print, radio, online and TV, are convinced of exiled media's continued need wherever they are based. "Myanmar's still a military-dominated state, and there's still a role for the exile media," insists Brian Joseph, NED's senior director for Asia. He says exile outlets can—and should—still play an important role in the overall development of independent media in Myanmar.

But funding is already a problem. Take DVB. In 2010, 16 donors stumped up $4.5 million. Last year, that dropped to $3.2 million from 13 donors. This year may be worse, thanks in no small part to an embezzlement scandal. A crucial annual donor meeting is scheduled for next month in Bangkok. Managing editor Khin Maung Soe is optimistic. "Some donors like to think Myanmar is changing very quickly and want us to move back, but the problem is, the government is not happy to allow us," he said, adding without irony, "Who will cover corruption while censorship still exists?" Across town, the *Irrawaddy* is also struggling to secure its $1 million annual budget. It published its final quarterly magazine last month and is now online only. Staff numbers have been cut from a 2011 high of 65 to the current 45. The editor thinks they can meet 80% of the previous year's budget in 2012. Beyond that, its donor-dependent business model looks vulnerable. Both the *Irrawaddy* and DVB confirmed they have attracted investment interest from within Myanmar. "I've had offers from tycoons, they want my brand" says Aung Zaw. "There are people who talk to me—'How much do you need?' I'm offered a chopper, three of four vehicles.... But I don't make [a] decision. I don't want to lose our independent voice" (Jackson 2012).

5.4 MEDIA REFORMS

During the transition from military to quasi-civilian rule, censorship has eased informally, especially over economic matters and the opposition led by pro-democracy icon Aung San Suu Kyi, but there are still no-go areas for local reporters. All the while, journalists remain under threat of the Printer and Publisher Registration Act that was implemented after military takeover and that allows for imprisonment for "harming the ideology and views" of the government. The vague and arbitrary Ministry of Informaton's 12-point censorship policy still broadly bars any reporting on matters considered a threat to national unity or security.

The Minister of Information and Culture of Myanmar, Kyaw Hsan, stated on March 19, 2012, at a two-day conference on "Media Development in Myanmar," that his ministry has been implementing a three-step process of reform of media in the country through which press restrictions are gradually being relaxed. In the first step, he stated, "we are paving the way for domestic periodicals to practice press freedom with responsibility and accountability" in order for them "to work in harmony with the future print media law." The minister added, "because of these reforms today, 173 journals and 124 magazines can now publish without prior approval from the Press Scrutiny and Registration Department ...." (Burma: Minister Explains 3-Step 'Media Reform Process' at Conference, MIZZIMA NEWS (Mar. 20, 2012).

The second step is the process of drafting a new print media law to replace the 1962 Registration of Printers and Publishers Law and to ensure freedom of the press as guaranteed by the Constitution. Article 354(a) of the Constitution provides that every citizen shall be at liberty "to express and publish freely their convictions and opinions," provided it is not contrary to the country's laws, security, law and order, and public order and morality (Constitution of the Union of the Republic of Myanmar (2008)).

The third stage entails the Ministry of Information's oversight of the implementation of the new print media law as the private media exercise the freedoms and obligations set forth in it. The minister stated, "we are not drafting the new media law with the intention of banning or hampering press freedom. Our aim is to facilitate the proper use of press freedom for the long-term progress of Myanmar's media sector." Despite questioning of the government's right to supervise the media, he argued, "our goal is the emergence of current media reforms (and the) emergence of a genuine fourth estate in a democratic society" (Burma: Minister Explains 3-Step 'Media Reform Process' at Conference, *supra.*).

On January 30-31, the new media law, drafted by the Information Ministry's PSRD was introduced at a two-day media workshop jointly organized by the Myanmar Writers and Journalists Association and Singapore-based Asia Media Information and Communication Centre (AMIC). The Information Ministry has drawn the draft from July to December 2011 and sent the first draft to the Union Attorney-General Office in January 2012. Then, the process went on with the second draft in April 2012, the third draft in May 2012, the fourth and fifth draft in June 2012 respectively. The draft media law was sent to the President Office in June 2012 and accepted the advices of the legal advisory group of the President in July 2012. The Information Ministry and the Union Attorney-General Office are in coordination with each other to complete the bill. They confirmed that the bill will be introduced to the ongoing Parliament soon after seeking authorization from the President Office.

On August 1, 2012, 92 journalists from Myanmar Journalists' Association (MJA), Myanmar Journalists' Network (MJN) and Myanmar Journalists' Union (MJU) held a meeting at the Royal Rose Garden in Yangon. A demonstration by a number of journalists wearing black T-shirts decorated with the catchphrase 'STOP KILLING PRESS' was launched in former capital Rangoon on 4 August 2012 to go up against the suspension of two journals—*Envoy* and the *Voice Weekly*. According to the PSRD, it met with the publisher and the editor of the *Envoy Journal* on 5 May, 2012, and the *Voice Weekly* journal on 18 June, 2012, and instructed them to follow the directives of the central supervisory committee. The PSRD said it had no alternative but to suspend the two weekly journals for two weeks as they broke the instructions of the department again, the paper reported. This led to large-scale opposition amid fears that PSRD bureaucrats are returning to strict draconian censorship laws.

Myanmar Government released its Notification No. 61/2012 on 9 August 2012 stating the 'Formation of Myanmar Core Press Council' (MCPC) which consists of 20 members. The council's key tasks are to protect media officials, to take responsibility for the compilation of journalistic code of ethics and to settle press disputes in accordance with rules and regulations laid out under Sub-Section (A) of Section 354 of the Constitution (Constitution 2008). It also states that, before the emergence of Press Media Laws, members of the media will be permitted to freely express and publish their convictions and opinions, so long as they are not contrary to the law. The Press Media Laws will be approved by the Union Parliament in due course (NLM 2012, August 11).

According to the state-run media, the Myanmar Core Press Council has been formed with the following persons:

U Khin Maung Aye (Retd. Supreme Courte Judge) Chiarman

Dr Aung Tun Thet (Retd. Principal) Vice-Chairman-1, United Nations System Staff College

Dr Khin Aye (Maung Khin Min-Danubyu) Vice-Chairman-2 (Retd. Myanmarsar Professor)

Dr Myo Thant Tin (Literati) Member
Dr Tin Hlaing (Boe Hlaing) (Literati) Member
U Khin Maung Lay (Pho Thaukkya) Member
U Soe Thein (Maung Wuntha) Member
U Thiha Saw (Thiha Saw) Member
U Aung Hla Tun (Reuters) Member
U Tin Hlaing (Ledwintha Saw Chit) Member
U Khin Maung Tun (Khin Maung Tun-Lanmadaw) Member
U Ohn Maung (Myinmu Maung Naing Moe) Member
Daw Cho Cho Tin (Ma Sanda) Member
Dr Tin Tun Oo Member
Dr Tha Tun Oo (Today Media) Member
U Myint Maung Member
U Maung Maung Myint Aye Member
U Ko Ko (Ko Ko-Setmu Tekkatho) Secretary
U Maung Maung Oo (Hein Latt) Joint Secretary-1
Dr Kyaw Zaw Naing (Copy Rights Lawyer) Joint Secretary-2

The statement also expresses the duties and responsibilities of members of the core press council. They are to safeguard freedom of the press in accordance with the law; to supervise the expressions of members of the press such that their expressions are not detrimental to the interest of the people, the dignity of the state and national sovereignty; to settle disputes and complaints among members of the press as well as with those from outside the industry in line with established rules, regulations and codes of conduct; to act as a liaison between the people, the government and the press; to compile and prescribe the code of ethics for members of the press; to train and educate members of the press so that they employ the best journalistic practices; to try to improve capacity and standards of members of the press; to scrutinize imported periodicals and publications to confirm that they are in conformity with national interests.

Authorized powers of members of the core press council are named in notification No. 61/2012. They are tasked with compiling regulations and procedures of the Press Council and are permitted to freely develop the industry. These powers are also responsible for establishing connections with international organizations. They are sanctioned to address the row of newsmen in collecting and writing news. They have power to summon and coordinate with journalists who are in violation of the code of ethics. According to the notification, these officials can also use their above-mentioned authority to collect evidence and to prescribe penal code, codes of civil procedure and tort law. The core members of press council even enjoy immunity from criminal or civil prosecution, as they are exercising duties and authority that have been unintentionally vested in them. The notification also says that they are advisers to the government concerning press affairs. Moreover, they have the power of taming and taking actions as necessary with the journalists who breached journalism ethics. Moreover, the council members have authority to coordinate with government departments concerning matters related to the Press Council. It also says that members are allowed to carry out training on national politics for development of press and human resources.

But, on the other hand, the 'Organizing Committee for Myanmar Journalists Association' released a statement dated 10 August objecting that some of the points were improper for the press council (Lynn 2012). It says that "Duties and responsibilities of MCPC" and "Authorities of MCPC" not only failed to protect the 'Rights of Journalists' but also systematically limited the media personnel's routine careers. If those inappropriate rules and regulations are not removed, they will not support the MCPC, the statement said.

On the same day, the Eleven Media Group (EMG) also released their position towards the 'Formation of Myanmar Core Press Council'. EMG's criticism of the core press council is that the members are former core executives of the junta-backed Myanmar Writers and Journalists Association (MWJA), who are pro-government and have business interests in the media sector. Appointing them as press council members constitutes a conflict of interest. EMG also criticized an item under 'Duties and responsibilities of MCPC' as unacceptable. It states that "to supervise the expressions of those from the press field so that their expressions are not detrimental to the interest of the people, the dignity of the State and national sovereignty" is not only a veto on publications but also a ban on freedom of speech.

The government of Myanmar announced on August 20, 2012 that it would no longer censor private publications, a move that journalists described as a major step toward media freedom in a country where military governments have tried for decades to control the flow of information. The announcement was made to editors on Monday and posted on a government website. "All publications in Myanmar are exempt from the scrutiny of Press Scrutiny and Registration Department," the government said in a press statement (http://www.ministryofinformation.gov.mm/index.php). Private publications in Myanmar have been thriving since President Thein Sein began taking steps last year to open up the country's economy and move the country toward democracy. However, the 1962 Press Law will remain in place until a new Media Law is passed by Parliament sometime later this year.

The news media have been one of the most assertive sectors of Myanmar society since democratic reforms began 2011. Journalists have held protests against government interference in their work. Like the democratization process itself in Myanmar, the government has scaled back censorship gradually. In June 2011, articles dealing with entertainment, health, children and sports were taken off the list of subjects requiring prior censorship. In December 2011, economics, crime and legal affairs were removed. Education topics were taken off the list in March 2012. The only two topics remaining on the list—religion and politics—were freed from censorship in August 2012.

The recent and relative opening of the Burmese regime has resulted in information being more freely circulated on the Internet, despite continued close monitoring. The international community and Burmese human rights activists need to remain vigilant and keep striving for more freedom. Local journalists say the battle for true media freedom in Myanmar is far from over. While they no longer have to submit the articles to the state's Press Scrutiny and Registration Board, they can still be called on the carpet afterward if what they write offends the powerful. Articles still have to meet 16 guidelines, including a stipulation that media shouldn't harm national security or "the dignity of the state." Journalists say the issue of corruption—a sensitive topic given the obvious wealth the military elite have compiled in an otherwise very poor country—remains a particularly taboo topic. And despite the reforms, the Press Scrutiny and Registration Board still exist. The Electronics Act, which was used to prosecute and jail bloggers and "citizen journalists", also remains on the books.

However, there are some positive signs of momentum in the country. Journalists who were once forced to write about their country from exile are now welcome to travel to Myanmar and to interview its leaders. One of the main opposition news websites, Mizzima.com, now has a Rangoon office and prints a magazine distributed inside Myanmar, *M-ZINE*. Photos of opposition leader Aung San Suu Kyi—long banned—and articles that report approvingly on her National League for Democracy are now daily affair. Another positive development has been that foreign journalists who once had to sneak around Myanmar on tourist visas are now welcomed and given remarkable access to decision-makers. Although the pace of change has been remarkable in Myanmar, yet we have to wait and watch the courses of event to predict any real change happening in the country. According to Dr Ma Thida, human rights activist, "after nearly five decades of censorship, the news media is very immature.... Some still cannot differentiate between propaganda and media, some cannot separate activism and journalism".

Notes

1. The text reads as follows:

   The Central Registration Board hereby informs all printers and publishers that it has laid down the following principles to be adhered to in scrutinizing political, economic, and religious manuscripts, and novels, journals, and magazines. They must be scrutinized to see whether or not they contain:

   1. anything detrimental to the Burmese Socialist Program;
   2. anything detrimental to the ideology of the state;
   3. anything detrimental to the socialist economy;
   4. anything which might be harmful to national solidarity and unity;
   5. anything which might be harmful to security, the rule of law, peace, and public order;
   6. any incorrect ideas and opinions which do not accord with the times;
   7. any descriptions which, though factually correct, are unsuitable because of the time or the circumstances of their writing;
   8. any obscene (pornographic) writing;
   9. any writing which would encourage crimes and unnatural cruelty and violence;
   10. any criticism of a non-constructive type of the work of government departments;
   11. any libel or slander of any individual.

2. The State Peace and Development Council Law No. 5/2004 titled The Electronic Transactions Law.

3. The State Law and Order Restoration Council Law No. 10/96 titled The Computer Science Development Law.

4. The State Law and Order Restoration Council Law No. 8/96 titled The Television and Video Law.

Chapter 6

Conclusion

Mass media plays a substantive role in the formation of public opinion in a society and in shaping public policy and public action on major social, political and economic issues. This role of the mass media depends upon the degree of independent role played by the newspaper, television and radio in the society. This, in turn, depends upon the political system and practice that prevails in the country under study. This study addresses the question of inter-relationship of mass media with the authority structure of country. The example of autocratic political framework in Myanmar has been taken as a model for understanding the role of mass media in a typically restricted and brutalized record of freedom of expression in an authoritarian regime.

Since each society controls its mass media in accordance with its policies and needs, it formulates its own separate press theory. Therefore, media system that exists in a country is directly related to the political system in that country. The political system determines exact relationship between media and the government. In this regard, Siebert mentions about four theories of the world's national media of which authoritarian theory of Press best corresponds to the Burmese model of Press. However, beginning in June 2011, the authorities in Myanmar have been undertaking media reforms prior to the consideration of a new media law in Parliament. According to figures from the ministry, there are about 200 privately run journals and over 200 magazines published in

Myanmar. In the print media sector, there are five state-run newspapers: *Myanma Alin, the Mirror, New Light of Myanmar, Myawaddy* and *Yadanapon.*

6.1 SUMMARY AND VALIDATION OF THE HYPOTHESIS

The main objective of this book is to study the character of mass media in an authoritarian state. The study also seeks to explore various theories of media and its application in the case of Myanmar. Another empirical issue which the study outlines is about the role of mass media in pressurizing and creating awareness in the international community about the authoritarian structure of the regime in Myanmar. Finally, the purpose is to study the responsibility of mass media in setting the agenda for reforms after transition from authoritarianism to democracy. With the aforesaid goal in the background, the study sought to explore the following research questions. How far does the mass media help in understanding the social and political fabric of a nation? To what extent authority structure of a regime determines the framework of mass media in a country? What has been the impact of mass media in persuading the international community for reforms within Myanmar? Does the mass media set the agenda of political debate and reforms after democratization?

A review of the literature on politics and society in Myanmar has enabled an understanding of the social and political fabric of the nation. Here, particularly, print media has played a significant role validating the first argument in the hypothesis of the study. Although the publishing within Myanmar was highly restricted and circumscribed during military regime, yet the publications that have come out from scholars, academicians and activists working outside the country have been commendable and praiseworthy. These literatures in the form of books, magazines, research papers, monographs, novels, newspaper articles and online publishing are noteworthy. They have helped in understanding of the autocratic military framework and socio-political roots of authoritarianism in Myanmar. Media has provided an insight into different phases of military rule under different nomenclatures since 1962. The rule pattern of the government reflective of the prevailing political culture was particularly based on organic notion of the state which developed over the years even before the British rule and they continued after independence. This authoritarian nature of the state was based on highly personalized concept of power and authority. Although parliamentary democracy established after independence did not seek to develop the country from below, yet it was superficially rooted in the Burmese political culture and society. They reverted back to the authoritarian system in 1962 and patrimonial nature of state and authority has existed in Myanmar since then.

The importance of authoritarian institutions such as party, military, and state apparatus, in sustaining authoritarian rule is significant. In this regard, authority structure of the regime in Myanmar validates the second hypothesis relating to the framework of mass media in the country. Since last five decades, military in Myanmar has used its institution of control—the army, police, Special Branch, Military Intelligence (Sa Ya Ka) and the military-backed Union Solidarity and Development Association (USDA-predecessor of USDP) and its wide network of informers to repress and generate fear among those journalists who dare to speak out against the governments' policies, referendum of the Constitution. In 2007, during the violent crackdown against the monks and citizen (popularly known as saffron revolution) journalists were stopped from taking photographs of the protests and were issued a command to destroy cameras. Japanese photographer (Kenji Nagai) was shot dead. Furthermore, as the referendum to the 2008 Constitution drew closer, greater restrictions were imposed. Journalists inspected that they were being watched, followed and their activities being monitored. Various security agencies including the Special Branch Police and military in plain clothes normally visited areas of potential dissent such as tea houses, guest houses, markets and shops monitoring the conversation taking place and collecting intelligence from informers. In Myanmar, government surveillance by a variety of formal and informal security structures, as well as mass based organizations such as the

USDA, is so omnipresent that most Burmese are too afraid to utter any critical opinion of the government in public. They know that security forces may question them about conversations and they risk arrest and imprisonment for speaking critically about government. In such a climate of fear and surveillance, free and open discussion about referendum and draft Constitution was impossible.

Freedom of association and assembly is sharply restricted in Myanmar by a range of laws, as well as the police and military actions to disperse any public gatherings deemed to be anti-government. The colonial era Unlawful Association Act (1908) remains in force. SLORC Order No. 2/88 bans gathering walking, marching in processions, chanting slogans, delivering speeches, agitating and creating disturbances, on the streets by a group of five or more people regardless of whether the act is with the intention of creating a disturbance or of committing a crime or not. Despite severe restrictions, activists found protesting against the 2008 referendum were arrested and detained, many of whom are still under custody.

The third hypothesis relating to the role of impact of mass media in persuading the international community for reforms within Myanmar has been proved particularly in the context of clash between Western ideas of democracy and the military rule that disputed the result of the 1990 elections. This has made Myanmar a focus of international relations; at the center of which is Nobel laureate Aung San Suu Kyi, who over the years has evolved into an icon of democracy in the Western media. For that reason, Western support for democracy in Myanmar has since become inseparable from the name of Aung San Suu Kyi, and by extension, the NLD despite a prolonged period of house arrest separating her presence from the NLD and Myanmar society at large. Myanmar has been an international media flash point on and off, and a persistent point of contention in international relations since then. Besides, the Saffron Revolution and Internet enabled global support appears to have weakened the military junta's control of the nation.

The tropical storm that wreaked havoc in the Ayeyarwardy Delta in May 2008 put Myanmar back into the international headlines. The generally negative response from the international media to the announcement of the national referendum by the government of Myanmar three months earlier seemed to have given the military leaders reasons to be alarmed about unwanted interference in internal affairs; hence vindicating, from where they were standing, their reluctance to engage in speedy and unrestricted cooperation with international relief agencies. Timing, however, could not have been more sensitive for the military rulers, as the country was scheduled to hold a referendum on a newly drafted Constitution in just a matter of days after the cyclone struck, and the military regime was determined to keep the event under control. Western powers including the United States and the EU acted in concert, with some member states pushing for a UN resolution in order to force Myanmar to open its ports to foreign aid and threatening to invoke the UN "responsibility to protect" in the event of a failure to comply on the part of the military rulers. Condemnations of the military government for their foot-dragging over humanitarian aid, meanwhile, mounted in the international media. Events in Myanmar have taken their own course irrespective of international pressure, as the country's rulers have, somewhat ironically, availed themselves of the current state of international isolation. Amid condemnations of the military rulers for their alleged slow response to international offers of post-cyclone relief, Myanmar adopted a new Constitution in a national referendum.

In the years following the 1990, elections the Myanmar Lobby outside the country, with considerable sway over politicians in Western countries, has similarly pursued a campaign with one simple message: "The military government is bad, Aung San Suu Kyi is good." This good versus bad narrative, while serving to sideline unorthodox views, has helped essentially focus and simplify policy-making vis-à-vis Myanmar. The Western media campaigns and sanctions have achieved significant result in inducing the change that the West would like to see in Myanmar.

A short case study of the so-called Saffron Revolution in Myanmar can help to highlight the principles discussed above about the links between governance and journalism. The Burmese government attracted intense media attention for its repression of anti-government demonstrations by students and political activists in August 2007 and by Buddhist monks and their lay supporters in September 2007. In an attempt to control information, Myanmar's military junta relied more on harassing journalists and tightening their grip on 'old' communications technologies than obstructing the use of newer technologies. The regime warned journalists not to cover the demonstrations, tightened official censorship, increased its surveillance of journalists, and blocked telephone lines to the key news sources—the student leaders, opposition politicians and monasteries. The crackdown rapidly escalated after September 25, with one Japanese journalist being gunned down by a soldier, and approximately 15 Burmese journalists arrested. Despite high-intensity international media coverage, Myanmar's junta was slow to block newer technologies, only severing Internet services, most mobile/cellular telephone connections and landline connections out of the country on a widespread scale on September 28. Despite the disruption to these services, the images and stories continued to trickle out to the world, often due to activists smuggling information across the border into Thailand.

Myanmar rarely jams international radio or satellite television services, and instead relies on counter-propaganda. In what might be regarded as a serious misappropriation of development and Asian values rhetoric, *The New Light of Myanmar* newspaper attempted to smear foreign news services, particularly the British Broadcasting Corporation and Voice of America. "Saboteurs from inside and outside the nation and some foreign radio stations, which are jealous of national peace and development, have been making instigative acts through lies to cause internal instability and civil commotion," the newspaper reported. The first and most obvious lesson to be drawn from this example is the way in which the Burmese junta attempted to crush the important watchdog and agenda-setting activities of journalism. Media reports flagged the serious failures in development processes in Myanmar, where the military grow richer while citizens suffer manifest distress due to the decline in the long-stagnant economy and the crippling inflation that followed the junta's removal of fuel subsidies in August 2007. Although the junta did restrict the flow of international news, the paramount priority was dampening the Burmese civil society by censoring local media and targeting news sources, reporters and editors. The Internet, mobile telephones and other new communications technologies greatly assisted in informing, arousing and mobilizing communities within and outside Myanmar, although the use of new technologies was not essential to this process. The Burmese, in common with citizens of many Asian nations, have proved creative at circumventing censorship by smuggling older technologies—such as videos, tapes, facsimiles, photographs, and printed materials—within and beyond the nation. The real contribution of newer technologies is speedier transmission. Rapid transmission helps to capture public attention as 'hot' news erupts, and to create a mutually reinforcing cycle in which prompt and continuous updates about civil society activity intensify the already fiery pace of citizens' democratic (and very newsworthy) activity.

Finally, the last hypothesis stands validated when we study the role of media as agenda setter, paving the way towards democratization in Myanmar. The recent attempts to reform the media by liberalizing the restrictions and establishment of a provisional Press Council of Myanmar for drafting a new media law has been regarded as a significant development in the path of transition and change. The Burmese case also indicates that journalism's watch-dog function of sounding the alarm about problems in government will do little to help nations where civil society and the checks and balances of misappropriation of power are weak. Journalists provided startling coverage of the earlier weeks of the first Myanmar uprising of 1988, with little impact on the final outcome.

While authoritarian regimes would prefer to conduct repressive acts in secrecy, transparency alone will not empower local civil societies or global agencies to prevent their misdeeds. The media coverage could, in fact, have harmed democratic actors. Myanmar's junta is recorded as having used images and stories from the media to help identify and punish participants in demonstrations and other democratic activities. The Burmese junta's behavior is an extreme example of the intense repression that some Asian governments will impose on journalists who do not follow their preferred models of professional practice, particularly when the nation is at flash point. Asian governments have proved intolerant even of development journalists who did not fit their preferred mode of operation. The Indonesian government of then President Suharto displayed this during the mid-1990s, when it was increasing the number of permits allowed for Western correspondents at an exponential rate, but banned Inter Press correspondents from the country. Although the Suharto government espoused development journalism, it insisted on a government-as-press-partner interpretation. Inter Press's emancipatory journalism model was confronting, and in fact more so than the liberal watchdog model of the Western journalists.

6.2 CONCLUDING REMARKS

It can be concluded that media in Myanmar has seen a complete 'U-turn beginning with the complete press freedom during the era of Parliamentary democracy under U Nu. There were around three dozen newspapers, including English, Chinese and Hindi dailies under a civilian government. Journalists were free to set up relations with international press agencies. The establishment of military rule under Ne Win in 1962 led to the establishment of a completely restricted and highly controlled media regime in Myanmar. The PSRD and the authoritarian model of mass media brought about a total control over the press freedom in Myanmar. The Printers and Publishers Registration Law was introduced shortly after the 1962 military coup. After the 1988 people's uprising, the junta introduced more media restrictions such as the 1996 Television and Video Act, the 1996 Computer Science Development Act, the 2002 Wide Area Network Order and the 2004 Electronics Transactions Law. Time and again activists and international community has advocated the government to repeal restrictive laws including the 1962 Printers and Publishers Registration Act and the 2004 Electronics Act—described as vague and draconian legislation that has been used to jail journalists and curb Internet freedoms.

In a major reform initiative, the government has abolished pre-publication censorship of the country's media after a span of nearly five decades. The move does away with the earlier practice of submitting news reports and articles for vetting to the country's Press Scrutiny and Registration Department prior to publication. It marks a significant departure from the previous military regime that used strict censorship to curtail criticism of the junta and its policies. However, the earlier restrictive laws still remain in force and the existing media organizations have resorted to self censorship in fear of 'being inked' and 'ripped out' in the words of Anna Allot.

Chapter 7

Bibliography

7.1 PRIMARY SOURCES

BSPP (1964), *System of Correlation of Man and Environment*, third edition, Rangoon: Burma Socialist Programme Party. Online Edition. Accessed on October 19, 2008. URL: http://www.burmalibrary.org/docs/System-of-correlation.htm

Burmese Way to Socialism—BWS (1962), Published by the Information Department for the Revolutionary Council. Online Edition. Accessed on October 19, 2008. URL: http://www.burmalibrary.org/docs/The_Burmese_Way_to_Socialism.htm

Constitutional Principles Approved by the National Convention. Online edition. Accessed on October, 2008. URL: http://www.blc-burma.org/pdf/Constitution/bmic.pdf

Constitutional Principles Approved by the National Convention. Online edition. Accessed on October, 2008. URL: http://www.blc-burma.org/pdf/Constitution/bmic.pdf

Notification 7/2011, Self-Adminstered Divisions and Self-Administered Zones Announced, EBO, Election Monitor No. 12.

Printers and Publishers Registration Law 1962. Law No. 1 amended by the Revolutionary Council of the Union of Myanmar, 1971. Online Edition. URL: http://www.burmalibrary.org/docs6/Printers_and_Publishers_Registation_Act.pdf

Pyithu Hluttaw Election Law, SPDC Law No. 1/2010. Online edition. Accessed on May 21, 2010. URL: http://www.burmalibrary.org/docs08/Announcement_1-2010.pdf

Pyithu Hluttaw Election Law, SPDC Law No. 2/2010. Online edition. Accessed on May 21, 2010. URL: http://www.burmalibrary.org/docs08/Announcement_2-2010.pdf

Pyithu Hluttaw Election Law, SPDC Law No. 3/2010. Online edition. Accessed on May 21, 2010. URL: http://www.networkmyanmar.org/images/stories/PDF3/l3b.pdf

SLORC Declaration No. 1/90 of July 27, 1990. Accessed on October 14, 2008. URL: http://www.burmalibrary.org/docs/Declaration_1-90.htm

SPDC Constitution — Online edition. Accessed on October, 2008. URL: http://d.scribd.com/docs/1sa6nutywy63lve274w2.pdf

The Burma Citizenship Law 1982, Pyithu Hluttaw Law No. 4 of 1982, Online Edition. URL: http://www.ibiblio.org/obl/docs/Citizenship%20Law.htm

The Computer Science Development Law. The State Law and Order Restoration Council Law No. 10/96 Online Edition. URL: http://www.blc-burma.org/html/myanmar%20law/lr_e_ml96_10.html

The Constitution of 'The Socialist Republic of the Union of Burma,' 1974. Online edition. Accessed on September 10, 2008. URL: http://www.thailawforum.com/database1/constmyanmar.html

The Constitution of BSPP for the transitional period of its Construction adopted by the Revolutionary Council, 1962. Online Edition. Accessed on October 19, 2008. URL: http://www.burmalibrary.org/docs/BSPP_CONSTITUTION.htm

The Constitution of the 'Union of Burma' 1947. Online edition. Accessed on September 10, 2008. URL: http://www.blc-burma.org/html/Constitution/1947.html

The Electronic Transactions Law. The State Peace and Development Council Law No. 5/2004 Online Edition. URL: http://www.blc-burma.org/html/myanmar%20law/lr_e_ml04_05.htm

The Manifesto of the National League for Democracy on Multi-Party Democracy General Election. Accessed on October 31, 2008. URL: http://burmalibrary.org/docs/NLDElectionManifesto1989.htm

The Motion Picture Law. The State Law and Order Restoration Council Law No.9/96. Online Edition. URL: http://www.blc-burma.org/html/myanmar%20law/lr_e_ml96_09.html

The Panglong Agreement, 1947, Online edition. Accessed on September 10, 2008. URL: http://www.burmalibrary.org/docs/panglong_agreement.htm

The Television and Video Law. The State Law and Order Restoration Council Law No. 8/96. Online Edition. URL: http://www.blc-burma.org/html/myanmar%20law/lr_e_ml96_08.html

Union of Myanmar Commission for Holding the Referendum. — Announcement No 10/2008, Nay Pyi Taw, 15 May 2008. Online at: http://mission.itu.ch/MISSIONS/Myanmar/statement&speech/No%2010_2008%20Announcement%20for%20refrendum.htm

7.2 SECONDARY SOURCES

Alagappa, Muthiah (2001c), "Asian Civil Military Relations: Key Developments, Explanations, and Trajectories" in Muthiah Alagappa (ed). *Coercion and Governance: The Declining Political Role of the Military in Asia*, Stanford, California: Stanford University Press, pp. 433-98.

Alamgir, Jalal (1997), "Against the Current: The Survival of Authoritarianism in Burma", *Pacific Affairs*, Vol. 70(3), pp. 333-50.

Allott, Anna J. (1981), "Prose writing and Publishing in Burma Today—Government Policy and Popular Practice" in

Tham Seong Chee, ed. *Literature and Society in Southeast Asia*, 1-35. Singapore: University Press.

Allott, Anna J. (1993), *Inked Over, Ripped Out—Burmese Storytellers and the Censors*, PEN American Center.

Altsean (2011), Burma 2011: Still a Military Dictatorship, No. 1078, March 24. URL: http://www.altsean.org/Reports/Burma2011.php

Amnesty International (2010), *Myanmar's 2010 Elections: A Human Rights Perspective*, May 11. Online edition. Accessed on May 21, 2010. URL: http://www.amnesty.org/en/library/asset/ASA16/007/2010/en/923dd424-81c1-4f04-9743-b74894b9bad7/asa160072010en.pdf

Anderson, Benedict R. O'G. (1983), "Old State, New Society: Indonesia's New Order in Comparative Historical Perspective" *The Journal of Asian Studies*, Vol. 42(3), pp. 477-96.

Andreas Schedler (2010), "Authoritarianism's Last Line of Defense", Journal *of Democracy*, Volume 21 (1), pp. 69-80.

BBC (2012), "William Hague welcomes end of 'long darkness' in Burma", January 6. http://www.bbc.co.uk/news/world-south-asia-16450519

Bertil Lintner, "Access to Information: The Case of Burma," The Right to Know: Access to Information in Southeast Asia (Philippine Center for Investigative Journalism Publication: 2001), <http://www.asiapacificms.com/papers/pdf/burma_access_to_information.pdf>

Bissinger, Jared (2012), "Foreign Investment in Myanmar: A Resource Boom but a Development Bust?" *Contemporary Southeast Asia*, Vol. 34 (1). pp. 23-52.

BNI (2011), "Hobson's choice: Burma's 2010 Elections". Online Edition. Accessed on January 8, 2011. URL: http://www.kaladanpress.org/v3/images/stories/document/HobsonsChoice-Burmas-2010-Elections.pdf

Bowman, Vickey (2007), "The Political Situation in Myanmar", in Monique Skidmore and Trevor Wilson (eds), *Myanmar: The State Community and the*

Environment, Asia Pacific Press, Australian National University, pp. 1-17. Online edition. Accessed on January 15, 2009. URL: http://epress.anu.edu.au/myanmar/pdf/whole_book.pdf

Brooker, Paul (2000), *Non-Democratic Regimes: Theory, Government and Politics*, London: Macmillan.

Brooten, Lisa (2006), "Political Violence and Journalism in a Multiethnic State: A Case Study of Burma (Myanmar)", *Journal of Communication Inquiry*, Volume 30 Number 4, pp. 354-73.

Callahan, P. Mary (2001), "Burma: Soldiers as State Builders" in Muthiah Alagappa (ed). *Coercion and Governance: The Declining Political Role of the Military in Asia*, Stanford, California: Stanford University Press, pp. 417-29.

Callahan, P. Mary (2003), *Making Enemies: War and State Building in Burma*, Ithaca: Cornell University Press.

Carey, Peter (1997), "From Burma to Myanmar: Military Rule and the Struggle for Democracy", *Conflict Studies*, No. 304: 1-27.

Carothers, Thomas (2002), "The End of the Transition Paradigm," *Journal of Democracy*, Vol. 13(1). pp 5-21.

Case, William (2002), *Politics in Southeast Asia; Democracy or less*. Routledge Curzon: London, New York.

Cawson, Alan (1991), "Corporatism" in David Miller ed. *The Blackwell Encyclopaedia of political Thought*, Blackwell Publishers, pp. 104-05.

Chowdhury, Mridul (2008), *The Role of the Internet in Burma's Saffron Revolution*, Berkman Center Research Publication No. 2008-08.

Collier, David (1995), "Trajectory of a Concept: Corporatism in the Study of Latin American Politics" in Peter H. Smith ed. *Latin America in Comparative Perspective: New Approaches to Methods and Analysis*, Westview Press. pp. 135-62.

Davies, Mathew (2012), "The Perils of Incoherence: ASEAN, Myanmar and the Avoidable Failures of Human Rights

Socialization?", *Contemporary Southeast Asia*, Vol. 34 (1). pp. 23-52.

Democratic Voice of Burma (2011), "Ex-army captain sentenced to 10 years", August, 29. http://www.dvb.no/news/ex-army-captain-sentenced-to-10-years/17316

Diamond Larry (2000), "The Global State of Democracy", *Current History*, Vol. 99 (641), December, pp. 413-18.

Diamond Larry et al. (1990), "Introduction: Comparing Experiences with Democracy", in Diamond et al. (eds.) *Politics in Developing Countries: Comparing Experiences with Democracy*, Boulder, London, Lynne Reinner Publishers.

Diamond, Larry (2008a), *The Spirit of Democracy*, Macmillan Publishers.

Diller, Janelle M. (1993), "Constitutional Reform in a Repressive State: The Case of Burma", *Asian Survey*, Vol. 33, No. 4, pp. 393-407.

Donald M. Seekins (2009), "Myanmar in 2008: Hardship, Compounded", *Asian Survey*, Vol. 49, No. 1, pp. 166-73.

Donald M. Seekins (2010), "Myanmar in 2009: A New Political Era?", *Asian Survey*, Vol. 50, No. 1, pp. 195-202.

Du, Roseline Ying (2008), *Mass Media's Agenda Setting Function in the Age of Globalization: A Multi-National Agenda-Setting Test*, Ph.D dissertation, University of North Carolina, School of Journalism and Mass Communication.

EBO (2011), "The Burma Army's Offensive Against the Shan State Army—North", Analysis Paper No. 3.

Ferguson, Jane N. (2008), "Revolutionary Scripts: Shan Insurgents Media Practice at Thai Burma Border", in Krishna Sen, Terence Lee (eds.) *Political Regimes and the Media in Asia*, Volume 12 of *Media, Culture, and Social change in Asia Series*, Routledge.

Finer, S.E. (1962), "The Man on Horseback: The Role of Military in the Politics", Harmondsworth: Penguin. Quoted in Brooker, Paul (2000), *Non-Democratic*

Regimes: Theory, Government and Politics, London: Macmillan.

Fink, Christina (2001), *Living Silence: Burma Under Military Rule*, London, New York: Zed Books.

Ganesan, N. Kyaw Yin Hlaing (2007), *Myanmar: State, Society and Ethnicity*, ISEAS.

Ghosh, Jayati (1996), "Coercive Corporatism: The State in Indonesian Capitalism", *Social Scientist*, Vol. 24(11-12), pp. 36-49.

Gill, Graeme (2000), *The Dynamics of Democratisation: Elites, Civil Society and the Transition Process*, Macmillan.

Goodwin, Barbara (2007), *Using Political Ideas*, John Willey and Sons, 5th Edition. First published in 1982.

Gravers, Mikael (1993), *Nationalism as Political Paranoia in Burma: An Essay on the Historical Practice of Power*, NIAS.

Guyot, James (1998), "Burma in 1997", *Asian Survey*, Vol. 32 (2), pp. 190-95.

Gyi, Maung Maung (1983), *Burmese Political Values: The Socio-political Roots of Authoritarianism*, New York: Preager.

Haacke, Jürgen (2010), "Myanmar's 2010 Elections and International Legitimacy: A Perspective on ASEAN's Stance vis-à-vis Naypitaw", in Levenstein, Susan L. eds., Finding Dollars, Sense and Legitimacy in Burma, Woodrow Wilson International Centre. Online edition. Accessed on May 18, 2011. URL:http://www.wilsoncenter.org/topics/pubs/ASIA_092010_Burma_rpt_for%20web.pdf

Hadiz, Vedi R. (2004a), "The Rise of Neo-Third Worldism? The Indonesian Trajectory and the Consolidation of Illiberal Democracy", *Third World Quarterly*, Vol. 25(1), pp. 55-71.

Hadiz, Vedi R. (2004b), "Indonesian Local Party Politics: A Site of Resistance to Neoliberal Reform", *Critical Asian Studies*, Vol. 36 (4), pp. 615-36.

Heywood, Andrew (2002), *Politics*, Palgrave, Macmillan.

Hlaing, Kyaw Yin (2008), "Power and Factional Struggles in Post-independence Burmese Government", *Journal of Southeast Asian Studies*, Vol. 39 (1), pp. 149-77.

Horton, Guy (2005), *Dying Alive: A Legal Assessment of Human Rights Violation in Burma*, A Report funded by Netherlands Ministry for Development and Cooperation.

HRW (2008), "Vote to Nowhere: The May 2008 Constitutional Referendum in Burma", Accessed on October 31, 2008. URL:http://www.hrw.org/en/reports/2008/04/30/vote-nowhere

Hui, Chin (2012), Behind Myanmar's suspended Dam, China Dialogue. Online Edition. Accessed on 20 July 2012. URL: http://www.chinadialogue.net/article/show/single/en/4832

Human Rights Watch (2008), *Burma, Vote to Nowhere*, Human Rights Watch. Online Edition. URL: http://www.hrw.org/sites/default/files/reports/burma0508webwcover.pdf

Huntington, Samuel P. (1991), *The Third Wave: Democratisation in the Cate Twentieth Century*, Norman: University of California Press.

ICG (2008a), "Burma/ Myanmar After the Crackdown", Asia Report No. 144. Online Edition. URL: http://www.crisisgroup.org/~/media/Files/asia/south-east-asia/burma-myanmar/144_burma_myanmar_after_the_crackdown.ashx

ICG (2008b), "Burma/Myanmar After the Nargis", Asia Report No. 161. Online Edition. URL: http://www.crisisgroup.org/~/media/Files/asia/south-east-asia/burma-myanmar/161_burma_myanmar_after_nargis_time_to_normalise_aid_relations

ICG (2010), The Myanmar Election, *Asia Briefing* No. 105, Jakarta/Brussels, May 27. Accessed on May 29, 2010. URL: http://www.crisisgroup.org/en/regions/asia/south-east-asia/burma-myanmar/B105-the-myanmar-elections.aspx

ICG (2011a), Myanmar's Post Election Landscape, Briefing No. 118, 30 November. Online Edition. URL: http://www.crisisgroup.org/~/media/Files/asia/south-east-asia/burma-myanmar/B118%20Myanmars%20Post-Election%20Landscape.pdf

ICG (2011b), Myanmar: A New Peace Initiative, Asia Report No. 214, 30 November. Online Edition. URL: http://www.crisisgroup.org/~/media/Files/asia/south-east-asia/burma-myanmar/214%20Myanmar%20-%20A%20New%20Peace%20Initiative.pdf

ICG (2012), "Myanmar: The Politics of Economic Reform", *Asia Report* No. 231, 27 July. Online Edition. URL: http://www.crisisgroup.org/~/media/Files/asia/south-east-asia/burma-myanmar/231-myanmar-the-politics-of-economic-reform.pdf

Indian Express (2007), "Deep in jungle, generals feel safe in new capital: No Cellphones, no Net", October 5.

ITN (2007), Online Edition. Accessed on October 5, 2007. URL: http://itn.co.uk/news/d1c1d8458feb7eef71cac0647886559 7.html

Jackson, Joe (2012), "For Burma's Exiled Journalists, the Promise of Reform Brings Peril and Possibility", Time World. Online Edition. Accessed on 22 April 2012. URL: http://world.time.com/2012/03/02/for-burmas-exiled-journalists-the-promise-of-reform-brings-peril-and-possibility/#ixzz23VIiM5QC

Jagan, Larry (2008), "A Burmese Consolidation of Authoritarianism", *Himal*, Vol. 21 (6), pp. 17-19.

Jakarta Post (2011), "ASEAN gives Myanmar nod for 2014 chairmanship", November 18. Online Edition. URL: http://www.thejakartapost.com/news/2011/11/18/asean-gives-myanmar-nod-2014-chairmanship.html

Jakarta Times (2010), "Myanmar Cancels Voting in More Minority Areas", November 2. Online Edition. URL: http://www.thejakartapost.com/news/2010/11/02/myanmar-cancels-voting-more-minority-areas.html

Jurgen Habermas 1989 (1962). *The Structural Transformation of the Public Sphere*. Cambridge: Polity Press.

Katanyuu, Ruukun (2006), "Beyond Non-Interference in ASEAN: The Association's Role in Myanmar's National Reconciliation and Democratization" *Asian Survey*, November/December, Vol. 46(6): 825-45.

Ken, Maclean (2010), "The Rise of Private Indirect Government in Burma", in Levenstein, Susan L. eds, Finding Dollars, Sense and Legitimacy in Burma, Woodrow Wilson International Centre. Online edition. Accessed on May 18, 2011. URL: http://www.wilsoncenter.org/topics/pubs/ASIA_092010_Burma_rpt_for%20web.pdf

Kingston, Jeff (2008), "Burma's Despair", *Critical Asian Studies*, Vol. 40(1), pp. 3-43.

Kudo, Toshihiro, Fumiharo Mieno (2007), "Trade, Foreign Investment and Myanmar's Economic Development during the transition to an open economy", IDE, Discussion Paper. No. 116. Online Edition. URL: http://ir.ide.go.jp/dspace/bitstream/2344/624/3/ARRIDE_Discussion_No.116_kudo.pdf

Kyi, Aung San Suu (2011), World Economic Forum Annual Meeting in Davos. Online Edition. URL: http://www.weforum.org/news/aung-san-suu-kyi-addresses-world-economic-forum-annual-meeting-davos

Leehey, Jennifer (2005), "Writing in a Crazy Way" in Monique Skidmore (ed) *Burma at the Turn of the Twenty-first Century*, Honolulu: University of Hawaii Press, pp. 175-205.

Leifer, Michael (2001), "National Unity Party" in *Dictionary of Modern Politics of Southeast Asia*, London, New York: Routledge.

Levenstein, Susan L. eds (2010), Finding Dollars, Sense and Legitimacy in Burma, Woodrow Wilson International Centre. Online edition. Accessed on May 18, 2011. URL: http://www.wilsoncenter.org/topics/pubs/ASIA_092010_Burma_rpt_for%20web.pdf

Linz Juan J. and Alfred Stepan (1998), "Towards Consolidated Democracy" in Takashi Inoguchi (ed.), *The Changing Nature of Democracy*, Tokyo: United Nations University

Press. pp. 48-68. Quoted in Abubakar E. Hara (2001), "The Difficult Journey of Democratisation in Indonesia", *Contemporary Southeast Asia*, Vol. 23(2), August, pp. 307-26.

Linz, Juan J. (2000), *Totalitarian and Authoritarian Regimes*, London: Lynne Rienner Publishers.

Luwarso, Lukas (2000), "The Paradox of freedom in Southeast Asia." *Jakarta Post*, 3 May. Online Edition. Accessed on 7 September 2008. URL: www.inma.org/subscribers/papers/2003-Yin.doc

Lynn, Zin (2012), "Burma Creates 'Core Press Council' Amid Widespread Criticism", Online Edition. Accessed on 13 August 2012. URL: http://www.eurasiareview.com/12082012-burma-creates-core-press-council-amid-widespread-criticism-oped/

Malloy, J. (ed.) (1977), *Authoritarianism and Corporatism in Latin America*, Pittersburg: Pittersburg University Press. Quoted in in David Miller ed. *The Blackwell Encyclopaedia of Political Thought*, Blackwell Publishers.

Martin, F. Michael (2010), Burma's 2010 Elections: Implications of the New Constitution and Election Laws, Congressional Research Service. Accessed on November 30, 2010. URL: http://www.fas.org/sgp/crs/row/R41218.pdf

Maung Zarni (2000), "Resistance and Cybercommunities," In Ann De Vaney, Stephen Gance and Yan Ma (Eds.), *Digital Communications and New Coalitions Around the World*. New York: PETER LANG, pp. 71-88.

Maung, Mya (1997), "Burma's Economic Performance under Military Rule: An Assessment", *Asian Survey*, Vol. 37(6), pp. 503-24.

Mc Carthy, Stephen (2000), "Ten Years of Chaos in Burma: Foreign Investment and Economic Liberalization under the SLORC-SPDC, 1988 to 1998", *Pacific Affairs*, Vol. 73(2), pp. 233-62.

Mc Carthy, Stephen (2008), "Overturning the alms bowl: The price of survival and the consequences for political legitimacy in Burma", *Australian Journal of International Affairs*, Vol. 62(3), pp. 298-314.

Mc Cormick, John (1995), *Comparative Politics in Transition*, California: Wadsworth Publishing Company.

Mc Intyre, Andrew (1994), "Organising Interests: Corporatism in Indonesian Politics", Working Paper No. 43, Asia Research Paper. Accessed on August 28, 2008. URL: http://wwwarc.murdoch.edu.au/wp/WP43.pdf

Min Zin (2010), "Opposition Movements in Burma: The Question of Relevancy", in Levenstein, Susan L. eds., Finding Dollars, Sense and Legitimacy in Burma, Woodrow Wilson International Centre. Online edition. Accessed on May 18, 2011. URL: http://www.wilsoncenter.org/topics/pubs/ASIA_092010_Burma_rpt_for%20web.pdf

Mizzima (2008), "Media in Burma", January 23. Online Edition. URL: http://www.mizzima.com/programs/37-media-in-burma.html

Mizzima (2012), "Thein Sein gives a 'state of the Union' address to Parliament", March 1, Online edition. Accessed on April 24, 2012. URL: http://www.mizzima.com/news/inside-burma/6685-thein-sein-gives-a-state-of-the-union-address-to-parliament.html

Momayezi, Nasser (2006), "Totalitarianism", in Thomas M. Leonard ed., *Encyclopaedia of Developing World*, Routledge, pp. 1555-58.

Mutebi, Alex (2005), "Muddling Through Past Legacies: Myanmar's Civil Bureaucracy and the Need for Reform", in Kyaw Yin Hlaing, Robert H. Taylor and Tin Maung Maung Than (eds.), *Myanmar: Beyond Politics to Societal Imperatives*, ISEAS, pp. 140-60.

Myanmar Times (2012 "Censorship ends but free press uncertain", Volume 33(641), August 27-September 2. Online Edition. URL: http://www.mmtimes.com/2012/news/641/news03.html

Myay, Moe (2011), "Propaganda with New Media is required for Democratization in Burma", PPP 184: New Media and Democracy, Online Edition. URL:

http://www.asknetwork.org/knowledge-centre/research-paper/211-propaganda-with-new-media-is-required-for-democratization-in-burma.html

Myo Khin Ma Ma (2007), "Get Out", *Burma Digest,* August 25. Accessed on September 4, 2007. URL: http://burmadigest.info/2007/08/25/get-out/

NDI (2010) "Burma's 2010 Electoral Framework: A Legal and Human Rights Analysis", Accessed on November 29, 2010. URL: http://www.ndi.org/files/NDI_Burma_Elections_0810.pdf

New Light of Myanmar (2012), Formation of Core Press Council, August 11. Online Edition.

New York Times (2000), "By Deals with Burmese Junta, Minorities Thrive" Online Edition. Accessed on 10 November 2008. URL: http://query.nytimes.com/gst/fullpage.html?res=9500E7DE123BF934A25752C1A9669C8B63&sec=&spon=&pagewanted=all

Ng, May (2008), "Overturning the bowl", *Himal*, Vol. 21(3), pp. 56-59.

Norris, Pippa and Sina Odugbemi (2009), "Evaluating Media Performance", in Pippa Norris ed. *News Media and Governance Reform*, Washington DC, World Bank.

Pederson, Morten B. (2005), "The Chalenges of Transition in Myanmar", in Kyaw Yin Hlaing, Robert H. Taylor and Tin Maung Maung Than (eds), *Myanmar: Beyond Politics to Societal Imperatives*, ISEAS, pp. 161-84.

Perlmutter, Amos (1981), *Modern Authoritarianism*, New Haven, Conn.: Yale University Press.

Pinkney, Robert (2004), *Democracy in the Third World*, Lynne Rienner, CO USA.

Porter Donald J., (2002), *Managing Politics and Islam in Indonesia*, London and New York: Routledge Curzon.

Reporters Without Borders, Online Edition. Accessed on 10 March, 2012. URL: http://en.rsf.org/press-freedom-index-2011-2012,1043.html

Rieffel, Alexis (2010), *Myanmar/Burma: Inside Challenges, Outside Interests*, Brookings Institution Press.

Rod, Nancy Hudson (2008), "Not a Rice Eating Robot: Freedom to Speak in Burma", in Krishna Sen, Terence Lee (eds.) *Political Regimes and the Media in Asia*, Volume 12 of *Media, Culture, and Social Change in Asia Series*, Routledge.

Romano, Angela (2009), "Asia", in Pippa Norris (ed.), *News Media and Governance Reform*, Washington DC, World Bank.

Russell Hiang-Khng Heng (2002), "Introduction", in Russell Hiang-Khng Heng (ed), *Media Fortunes, Changing Times: ASEAN States in Transition*, Singapore: ISEAS.

Sarkin, Jeremy J. and Marek Pietschmann (2003), "Legitimate Humanitarian Intervention under International Law in the Context of the Current Human Rights and Humanitarian Crisis in Burma (Myanmar)" *Hong Kong Law Journal*, Vol. 33(2): p. 371.

Schedler, Andreas (2006), "The Logic of Electoral Authoritarianism" in Andreas Schedler (ed.), *Electoral Authoritarianism: The Dynamics of Unfree Competition*, Lynne Reinner.

Schmitter, P.C. (1974), "Still the Century of Corporatism", *Review of Politics*, Vol. 36, pp. 85-131.

Selth, Andrew (2010) "Modern Burma Studies: A Survey of the Field", *Modern Asian Studies*, Vol. 44(2). pp. 401-40.

Sen, Krishna (2008), "Mediating Political Transition in Asia" in Krishna Sen, Terence Lee (eds.) *Political Regimes and the Media in Asia, Volume 12 of Media, Culture, and Social Change in Asia Series*, Routledge.

Shin, Doh Chull (1994), "On the Third Wave of Democratisation: A Synthesis and Evaluation of Recent Theory and Research," *World Politics*, 47 (October), pp. 135-70. URL: http://links.jstor.org/sici?sici=0043-8871%28199410%2947%3A1%3C135%3AOTTWOD%3E2.0.CO%3B2-M

Siebert, Frederick S. et al. (1963), Four Theories of the Press: The Authoritarian, Libertarian, Social Responsibility, and Soviet Communist Concepts of What the Press Should Be and Do, University of Illinois Press.

Silverstein, Josef (1977), *Burma: Military Rule and the Politics of Stagnation*, Ithaca and London: Cornell University Press.

Singh, Udai Bhanu (2012), An Assessment of Manmohan Singh's visit to Myanmar, IDSA, Online Edition. Accessed on 5 July, 2012. URL: www.idsa.in/system/files/IB_ManmohanVisitMyanmar.pdf

Skidmore, Monique (2005), *Burma at the Turn of the Twenty-first Century*, Honolulu, University of Hawaii Press.

Sleth, Andrew (2008), "Burma's 'Saffron Revolution' and the Limits of International Influence", *Australian Journal of International Affairs*, Vol. 62(3), pp. 281-97.

Smith, Martin (1991), "State of Fear: Censorship in Burma (Myanmar)", Article 19, Country Report, Online Edition. URL: http://www.ibiblio.org/obl/docs3/State-of-Fear-minus.pdf

Smith, Martin (1995), "Censorship Prevails: Political Deadlock and Economic Transition in Burma", Article 19, Country Report, Online Edition. URL:

http://www.article19.org/data/files/pdfs/publications/burma-censorship-prevails.pdf

Smith, Martin (1999), *Burma: Insurgency and the Politics of Ethnicity*, London, New York, Dhaka: Zed Books.

Sorenson George (1998), *Democracy and Democratisation: Process and Prospects in a Changing World*, Boulder, Colorado: Westview Press.

South, Ashley (2004), "Political Transition in Myanmar", *Contemporary Southeast Asia*, Vol. 26 (2), pp. 233-55.

Steinberg David I. (1981), Burma's Road Toward Development: Growth and Ideology under Military Rule, Boulder, Colorado: Westview Press.

Steinberg David I. (1982), *Burma: A Socialist Nation of Southeast Asia*, Boulder, Colorado: Westview Press.

Steinberg, David I. (2001), *Burma: The State of Myanmar*, Washington DC: Georgetown University Press.

Steinberg, David I. (2003), "Myanmar: Reconciliation Progress in the Process?" *Southeast Asian Affairs* 2003, Singapore: Institute of Southeast Asian Studies, pp. 171-89.

Steinberg, David I. (2005), "Myanmar: The Roots of Economic Malaise", in Kyaw Yin Hlaing, Robert H. Taylor and Tin Maung Maung Than (eds), *Myanmar: Beyond Politics to Societal Imperatives*, ISEAS, pp. 86-116.

Steinberg, David I. (2006), "Civil Society and Legitimacy: The Basis of National Reconciliation in Myanmar", in Trevor Wilson (ed.), *Myanmar's Long Road to National Reconciliation*, ISEAS, pp. 149-76.

Steinberg, David I. (2010), *Burma/Myanmar: What Everyone Needs to Know*, Oxford University Press.

Sundhaussen, Ulf (1982), *The Road to Power: Indonesian Military Politics 1945-1967*, Oxford University Press.

Taylor, Robert H. (2005), "Pathways to the Present", in Kyaw Yin Hlaing, Robert H. Taylor and Tin Maung Maung Than (eds.), *Myanmar: Beyond Politics to Societal Imperatives*, ISEAS, pp. 1-29.

Telegraph (2012), "Hilary Clinton welcomes release of 651 political prisoners in Burma", January 13, http://www.telegraph.co.uk/news/worldnews/asia/burmamyanmar/9014278/Hilary-Clinton-welcomes-release-of-651-political-prisoners-in-Burma.html

Than, Tin Maun Maung (2002), "Myanmar Media: Meeting Market Challenges in the Shadow of the State", in Russell Hiang-Khng Heng (ed.), *Media Fortunes, Changing Times: ASEAN States in Transition*, Singapore: ISEAS, pp. 139-71.

Than, Tin Maung Maung (2007), *State Dominance in Myanmar: The Political economy of Industrialisation*, ISEAS.

Thant, Myint U (2001), *The Making of Modern Burma*, Cambridge University Press, Cambridge.

Thant, Myint U (2006), *The River of Lost Footsteps: Histories of Burma,* Farrer, Straus and Giroux, New York.

Thawnghmung, Ardeth Mung (2003), "Pre-conditions and Prospects for Democratic Transition in Myanmar", *Asian Survey*, Vol. XLIII(3), May/June, pp. 443-60.

TNI (2010), *A Changing Ethnic Landscape: Analysis of Burma's 2010 Polls*, Briefing No. 4. Online Edition. URL: http://www.tni.org/sites/www.tni.org/files/download/bpb4final.pdf

TNI (2011), "Burma's New Government: Prospects for Governance and Peace in Ethnic States", Policy Brief No. 6.

Turnell, Sean (2011), "Myanmar in 2010: Doors open Doors Close", *Asian Survey*, Vol. 51(1) pp. 148-54.

Turnell, Sean (2012), "Myanmar in 2011: Confounding Expectations", *Asian Survey*, Vol. 52(1), pp. 157-64.

Voice of America (2012), "French Foreign Minister meets Burmese opposition figure", January 15. http://www.voanews.com/tibetan-english/news/French-Foreign-Minister-Meets-Burmese-Opposition-Figure-137426608.html

Wilson, Trevor (2010), "Significance of Myanmar's 2010 Elections", *New Mandala*, December 15 URL: http://asiapacific.anu.edu.au/newmandala/2010/12/15/the-significance-of-myanmar%E2%80%99s-2010-election/

Wood, James (2000), "China and Southeast Asia", *History of International Broadcasting*, Volume 2, IEE Publication Series.

Zarni, Maung Maung (2010), "Why Soldiers Don't Rebel in Than Shwe's Burma", Irrawaddy, October 4. Online Edition. URL: http://www2.irrawaddy.org/print_article.php?art_id=19625

Zaw, Aung (2002), "In Burma, a Repressive Regime Controls the Press", in Melissa Ludtke ed., *Journalism in Asia,* Nieman Reports, Summer. Online Edition. URL: http://www.nieman.harvard.edu/reports/article/101377/In-Burma-a-Repressive-Regime-Controls-the-Press.aspx